scrumptious

cooking with **Lynn Bedford Hall**

Author's acknowledgements

No book of this kind ever sees the light of day without a lot of input from a lot of people, and never mind the author. These people all deserve a fat thank you starting with my family who, as always, had to eat and evaluate on the nights I was testing, and go hungry on the days I was writing. My gratitude, also, to Publishing Director Linda de Villiers for her wisdom, guidance and patient involvement from beginning to end. To Joy Clack, who edited the manuscript with great dedication and who had but one answer to all my requests: No Problem, a response which is every author's dream. And to Bev Dodd, who worked tirelessly to come up with this brilliant, exciting and innovative design. To them – and to everyone else on board – I thank you.

LYNN BEDFORD HALL, 1999

First published in 1999 by
Struik Publishers (Pty) Ltd (a member of Struik New Holland Publishing (Pty) Ltd)
Cornelis Struik House, 80 McKenzie Street, Cape Town 8001

Reg. No.: 54/00965/07

10 9 8 7 6 5

Editor: Joy Clack
Concept designer: Petal Palmer
Designer: Beverley Dodd
Photographer: Anthony Johnson
Stylist: Vo Pollard

Reproduction by Disc Express Cape (Pty) Ltd
Printed and bound by Craft Print (Pte) Ltd, Singapore

ISBN 1 86872 308 9

contents

 # spreads, dips and snacks ...

Elsa Maxwell was absolutely right when she said that **cocktail parties** were the worst invention since castor oil. Personally, I can think of no good reason for throwing one, unless you want to cross a lot of names off your guest list. Asking around, it seems that most people are ambivalent about these affairs, one reason being that when they finally get home they either have to make supper or go to bed full of little bits. The main objection, however, is that they happen at such an unfortunate time.

Being invited to a cocktail party means that you cannot unwind with a **sundowner** in front of your telly at the end of the day. Instead, you have to dress up and lock up in order to get somewhere by 6 pm. Having got there, you then have to stand in a room full of people and **animate** – with a glass in one hand, a sausage in the other and an elbow in your ribs. Often the people you're animating with are complete strangers, but I, for one, find it very difficult to break away. It seems so rude. "Excuse me but I've run out of things to say." And sometimes the room is so full that moving is impossible anyway. Once I spent an entire evening squashed into a bowl of proteas. Every time I tried to get away from the proteas I walked into a tray of meatballs on toothpicks. That was the evening I eventually left without even clapping eyes on my hosts. Perhaps they weren't even there. For all I know they might have gone to a movie. If they'd had any sense they would have gone to a movie.

There are times, however, when you want to have friends around without having a formal dinner party, and this is when you lay on a **spread of spreads**. You set them out on a table and let people help themselves. Pretty girls do not have to walk around carrying the tables, and you're never cornered into making small-talk with your mouth full of samoosa. People simply wander to the **buffet** when they're hungry, so the crowd keeps moving. And if you put a pile of plates at one end, things won't drip onto the carpet. The result can then be a long, relaxed and merry affair. The hostess will be merry too, because only a few of the suggested offerings require on-the-spot heating. At the end of the day, a good time should have been had by all.

... or how not to have a cocktail party

White Bean Dip with Tahini and Spices

This **dip** is not unlike **hummus,** but it contains **Italian beans,** instead of chickpeas, sizzled **spices** and **yoghurt**.

30 ml (2 tbsp) oil
1 medium onion, finely chopped
2 cloves garlic, crushed
5 ml (1 tsp) ground cumin
5 ml (1 tsp) ground coriander
2 ml (½ tsp) ground ginger
1 x 400 g (14 oz) can cannellini
   beans, drained and rinsed*
15 ml (1 tbsp) lemon juice
30 ml (2 tbsp) tahini
   (sesame seed paste)
75 ml (5 tbsp) thick
   Bulgarian yoghurt
5 ml (1 tsp) honey
salt to taste

Heat the oil in a small, deep saucepan and lightly sauté the onion and garlic. Add spices, stir and sizzle for a few seconds, then remove the pan from the stove. Add the beans and toss to mix. Spoon into a processor fitted with the metal blade, add remaining ingredients and blend well, stopping to scrape down the sides when necessary. The resulting purée should be creamy, but will not be absolutely smooth. Spoon into a glass jar, cover and refrigerate for a day, or overnight.

* These are small kidney beans, larger than haricots yet smaller than butter beans – available in cans.

Roasted Red Pepper, Chilli and Cheese Dip

2 large red peppers
125 g (4½ oz) smooth, low-fat
  cottage cheese (see p. 208)
15 ml (1 tbsp) thick, bright
  red chilli sauce
a pinch each of salt and sugar
a few drops of lemon juice
a few tufts of parsley
1 slice stale, crustless bread
30–45 ml (2–3 tbsp) fresh
  coriander leaves
a drizzle of olive oil and fresh
  coriander to garnish

Quarter peppers and remove core, thick inner membranes and seeds. Place on a rack, skin sides up, and grill until blackened and blistered. Wrap in a damp kitchen towel or in a brown paper bag, close, and leave until cool, then peel and chop roughly.

Place in a processor fitted with the metal blade, add the remaining ingredients and process until very well combined – the mixture should be slightly chunky, with a bright colour and studded with small bits of pepper. Spoon into a glass container, cover and refrigerate overnight. Garnish just before serving.

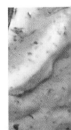

Best Brinjal Dip

If you've ever wondered why some **brinjal dips** have an unpleasant, sharp tang, it's the fault of the bitter juices that lurk inside **brinjals** and spoil the subtle flavour. That, and the raw garlic. Give this method a try – it solves both these problems and you'll be surprised at the difference in taste. The recipe is based on the standard Greek **Melitzanosalata**, with a few personal twists.

500 g (1 lb 2 oz) brinjals
2 cloves garlic, unpeeled
30 ml (2 tbsp) Greek yoghurt
10 ml (2 tsp) lemon juice
1 pickling-sized onion, chopped
5 ml (1 tsp) honey
2 ml (½ tsp) ground cumin
30 ml (2 tbsp) olive oil
salt to taste
black olives to garnish

Prick brinjals all over with a skewer, place on a baking tray lined with baking paper, and bake at 200 °C (400 °F, Gas Mark 6) for 45–50 minutes until soft and wrinkled. Add the cloves of garlic 10 minutes before the end of the baking time. When cool enough to handle, pull skin off brinjals, then gently squeeze the flesh between doubled sheets of paper towelling to remove the excess juices. At this stage it will look most unappetising, but never mind, just chop it up and put into a processor fitted with the metal blade. Snip the tips off the garlic and squeeze the pulp directly into the bowl, then add the remaining ingredients and process until smooth and creamy. Check seasoning, spoon mixture into a glass container, cover and refrigerate for several hours or overnight. Dot with a few olives before serving.

Creamy Feta and Herb Dip

200 g (7 oz) feta cheese, diced
125 ml (4½ fl oz) Greek yoghurt
a few drops of lemon juice
6 tufts of parsley
3–4 fresh basil leaves, roughly torn
15 ml (1 tbsp) chopped chives
15 ml (1 tbsp) olive oil
5 ml (1 tsp) honey
a pinch of salt
extra snipped chives or sun-dried
  tomatoes to garnish

Place all the ingredients in a processor fitted with the metal blade and process until thoroughly mixed, but not absolutely smooth – a few crumbles of feta should still be visible. Spoon the mixture into a glass container, cover and refrigerate overnight. Sprinkle with chives or dot with slivered tomatoes before serving.

Spicy Red Lentil Spread

These basic ingredients make a nourishing and enormous bowlful.

250 ml (180 g/6½ oz) red lentils,
rinsed
500 ml (18 fl oz) water
2 ml (½ tsp) each salt and paprika
15 ml (1 tbsp) each butter and oil
1 small onion, finely chopped
2 cloves garlic, crushed
7 ml (1½ tsp) curry powder
7 ml (1½ tsp) peeled, chopped
root ginger
2 medium tomatoes, skinned
and finely chopped
10 ml (2 tsp) lemon juice
a nut of butter
45 ml (3 tbsp) fresh coriander
leaves
salt to taste
roasted garam masala to garnish

Cover the base of a heavy saucepan with a thin film of oil, then add the lentils, water, salt and paprika. Bring to the boil and simmer, covered, for about 15 minutes or until soft. Keep the heat very low or the lentils will stick and burn. Set aside, uncovered – the lentils will absorb any excess moisture and turn into a thick 'porridge'. Heat the butter and oil, and sauté the onion and garlic with the curry powder and ginger. Add the tomatoes and simmer until completely soft, to make a thick sauce. Add the lentils and remaining ingredients and mash well, using a wooden spoon. Spoon the mixture into a glass container, cover and refrigerate for a day or overnight. Sprinkle with masala before serving.

Tuna and Butter Bean Spread

This is known as my Pleb Spread. Almost all the ingredients come out of either a can, a bottle or a jar. There's also some **bread** in it. And **fish paste**. The funny thing is, everyone seems to like it. Further bonuses are: this quantity makes plenty; it packs in a heap of nourishment; and, provided you don't garnish it with **butter beans**, nobody will guess what's inside.

1 x 150 g (5½ oz) can shredded
  tuna in oil, undrained
1 x 410 g (14 oz) can butter beans,
  well drained and patted dry
2 pickling-sized onions, chopped
15 ml (1 tbsp) lemon juice
45 ml (3 tbsp) thick mayonnaise
15 ml (1 tbsp) tomato sauce
5 ml (1 tsp) Worcestershire sauce
1 ml (¼ tsp) paprika
10 ml (2 tsp) anchovy paste
1 slice crustless bread, torn
  into pieces
salt to taste
olives, capers, anchovies, extra
  paprika – anything, really, except
  butter beans to garnish

Place all the ingredients in a processor fitted with the metal blade and process, scraping down the sides when necessary, until the mixture is smooth and creamy. Turn into a glass container, cover and refrigerate overnight. Garnish before serving.

Herbed Cream Cheese with Sun-dried Tomatoes and Walnuts

250 g (9 oz) cream cheese OR
smooth, low-fat cottage cheese
(see p. 208)

sun-dried tomatoes in oil, drained
and snipped to provide 60 ml
(4 tbsp)

6 large walnut halves, chopped

30 ml (2 tbsp) finely snipped chives

30 ml (2 tbsp) finely chopped
parsley

8 large basil leaves, snipped

15 ml (1 tbsp) mayonnaise

a little salt

Place all ingredients in a mixing bowl and stir together until

thoroughly blended. Spoon the mixture into a glass container,

cover and refrigerate for a few hours.

Double-quick Mushroom Pâté

Never any leftovers with this one.

250 g (9 oz) brown mushrooms,
  wiped and finely chopped
60 g (2 oz) butter, diced
1 large sprig rosemary
1 plump clove garlic, crushed
30 ml (2 tbsp) soy sauce
30 ml (2 tbsp) sweet sherry
1 medium onion, finely chopped
250 g (9 oz) smooth, low-fat
  cottage cheese (see p. 208)
chopped parsley to garnish

Place all the ingredients, except the cottage cheese, in a saucepan, cover and bring to a slow simmer, then uncover and cook, stirring, for about two minutes or until the onion and mushrooms are soft and the mixture is almost dry. Remove from the heat, discard rosemary sprig and allow mixture to cool before stirring it into the cottage cheese. Turn into a pottery serving dish, cover and refrigerate, preferably overnight.

Unfortunately the colour is a bit muddy and needs to be cheered up with a sprinkling of parsley before serving.

Black Olive Paste

Tapenade is a **black olive** paste from Provence, with a dozen uses – spread on bread or toast, on meat before roasting, on fish after baking, added to beefy stews or served with grilled vegetables... The olive-loving French will always fall on **tapenade**, but it can be quite pungent, so for those of us who don't enjoy an in-your-face **olive flavour**, here is a version that is not too intense.

about 200 g (7 oz) choice
   black olives
2 small cloves garlic, peeled
1 x 50 g (1¾ oz) can rolled fillets of
   anchovied sardines with capers
10–15 ml (2–3 tsp) fresh thyme
   leaves
2 slim spring onions, chopped
60 ml (4 tbsp) olive oil
10 ml (2 tsp) lemon juice
30 ml (2 tbsp) fine, fresh
   breadcrumbs

Stone olives and weigh – you need 140 g (5 oz) – then chop them roughly. Pour boiling water over the garlic, let it stand for one minute, then drain. Drain anchovies, but retrieve any capers that may fall out. Place olives, garlic, anchovies and capers, thyme and spring onions in a processor fitted with the metal blade and process, scraping down the sides when necessary, until finely chopped. Slowly add the oil and lemon juice and continue processing until well combined. If the mixture looks too oily, add the crumbs; if not, they can be left out. Spoon into a glass container, cover and refrigerate for a few hours or overnight.

Guacamole

There are as many versions of this **avocado dip** as there are cactuses in Mexico. Increase the **chillies**, add **cucumber**, add **celery** – short of adding a prickly pear, you simply can't go wrong. This is a tasty and reliable version.

1 firm but ripe avocado
(300 g/11 oz)
1 clove garlic, peeled and blanched
for one minute in boiling water
red chilli to taste, seeded and
chopped – start with 5 ml (1 tsp)
7 ml (1½ tsp) lemon juice
a few tufts of parsley
15 ml (1 tbsp) fresh coriander
leaves
15 ml (1 tbsp) finely chopped
red onion (if unavailable, use
spring onions)
1 small tomato, skinned, finely
chopped and seeded
a pinch each of salt and sugar
fresh coriander to garnish

Using an electric whisk, blend all the ingredients until well mixed but still slightly chunky. Spoon into a glass container, push the avocado pip into the middle (this helps to retain the colour), sprinkle with a little lemon juice, then cover and refrigerate for several hours. Remove pip and top with coriander leaves before serving.

Baby Marrow, Egg and Dill Pâté

An unusual pâté, light and elegant.

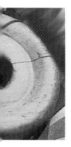

150 g (5½ oz) baby marrows,
   pared and sliced (prepared
   weight)
1 small onion, finely chopped
1 clove garlic, quartered
a few tufts of parsley
150 ml (5¼ fl oz) chicken or
   vegetable stock
1 bay leaf
a little salt
1 hard-boiled egg, chopped
5 ml (1 tsp) Dijon mustard
30 ml (2 tbsp) mayonnaise
milled black pepper
a large pinch of sugar
15 ml (1 tbsp) chopped fresh
   dill leaves
extra dill to garnish

Place marrows, onion, garlic, parsley, stock, bay leaf and salt in a large frying pan. Bring to the boil, then cover and simmer for about 20 minutes until marrows are very soft – you may have to add a little more stock, but all the liquid should be absorbed when done, otherwise drain. Cool, remove bay leaf, then tip into a processor fitted with the metal blade. Add the remaining ingredients and process, scraping down the sides when necessary, until mixture is creamy, lime-coloured and flecked with green. Check seasoning, spoon into a glass container, cover and refrigerate overnight. Sprinkle with chopped dill before serving.

Cocktail Chicken Wings

No grilling or basting required, just **marinate**, **bake**, and then pile these beautiful brown nibbles on a large platter for **snacking**.

1 kg (2¼ lb) chicken wings
   (about 16)
60 ml (4 tbsp) sweet sherry
30 ml (2 tbsp) tomato sauce
30 ml (2 tbsp) honey
60 ml (4 tbsp) soy sauce
30 ml (2 tbsp) lemon juice
30 ml (2 tbsp) oil
30 ml (2 tbsp) sesame seeds
2 plump cloves garlic, chopped
15 ml (1 tbsp) peeled, chopped
   root ginger
60 ml (4 tbsp) chicken stock

Remove wing tips and separate wings neatly at the joint without splintering the bone (you should end up with about 32 pieces). Place in a large baking dish (not a roasting tin) to fit closely together in a single layer. Place the remaining ingredients in a blender goblet and pulse to blend. Pour the mixture over the wings, toss until well coated, then leave to stand for 30 minutes. Bake, uncovered, at 180 °C (350 °F, Gas Mark 4) for 50–60 minutes until almost all the juices have evaporated and the wings are very brown and tender. Toss well with remaining juices, then transfer the wings to a platter and serve hot. Supply napkins.

Shrimp and Cheese Crostini

The **chunky topping** on these crisp little snacks is firm enough not to slither all over the place, and can be mixed and refrigerated in advance. The **bread rounds** can also be pre-prepared. Assemble and grill just prior to serving.

white or plain brown bread,
   not too fresh

TOPPING
125 g (4½ oz) cooked, peeled
   shrimps, coarsely chopped
125 ml (50 g/1¾ oz) grated
   Gruyère or Cheddar cheese
2 spring onions, chopped
5 ml (1 tsp) Dijon mustard
45 ml (3 tbsp) mayonnaise
2 ml (½ tsp) Worcestershire sauce
a little salt and milled black pepper

Using a 5 cm (2 in) scone cutter, stamp out 12–14 circles from

the bread and toast on one side only. To make the topping, mix

all the ingredients and spread on the untoasted side of each

bread round. Arrange on a baking tray, position well below the

grill, and grill until bubbling and the cheese has melted.

MAKES 12–14.

Crumbed Lemon and Garlic Cocktail Mussels

500 g (1 lb 2 oz) blanched,
   flash-frozen mussels on the
   half-shell (about 24)

TOPPING
60 ml (4 tbsp) olive oil
10 ml (2 tsp) butter
3–4 plump cloves garlic, crushed
10 ml (2 tsp) very finely grated
   lemon rind
250 ml (60 g/2 oz) fine, white,
   not-too-fresh breadcrumbs
30 ml (2 tbsp) finely chopped
   parsley
grated Parmesan cheese (optional)

There are different ways of preparing these mussels. Although they have been blanched, they have to be cooked before eating. I first thaw them in the refrigerator – they take a couple of hours. To make the topping, melt the oil, butter, garlic and lemon rind together, then mix into the crumbs and parsley. Loosen the mussels from their shells (for easy eating) and arrange them (still on the shells) in a shallow baking dish. Divide the moist crumb mixture between mussels, pressing on lightly – if using Parmesan, sprinkle a little over the tops at this stage. Bake in the centre of the oven at 200 °C (400 °F, Gas Mark 6) for about 12 minutes or until the crumbs are golden-brown and the mussels very hot (having had their second cooking). Serve immediately.

Pink Salmon and Anchovy Pâté

It's all in the title.

2 x 212 g (7 oz) cans
   pink salmon, drained
45–60 ml (3–4 tbsp) soft butter
60 ml (4 tbsp) olive oil
2 pickling-sized onions,
   coarsely grated
60 ml (4 tbsp) parsley,
   finely chopped
10 ml (2 tsp) lemon juice
1 ml (¼ tsp) each paprika
   and sugar
1 x 50 g (1¾ oz) can rolled fillets
   of anchovied sardines with
   capers, drained and chopped
10 ml (2 tsp) brandy

Remove any bones and bits of skin from the drained salmon,

then mash very well with remaining ingredients – use a wooden

spoon, not a blender. Spoon mixture into a glass container, cover

and refrigerate for several hours or overnight.

23

Pita Pizzas

The definitive short-cut pizza. Instead of making a base crust, simply buy ready-made **pita breads**, cover them with the topping of your choice and bake. Use traditional thin, flat pitas (either white or brown), and they shouldn't be too fresh. Spread the topping over the whole surface. A slick of pesto and/or snipped, sun-dried tomatoes make super additions. Slice into wedges before serving. These pitas are also good with soups, salads, or pasta dishes.

MUSHROOM AND MOZZARELLA TOPPING
250 g (9 oz) white mushrooms, wiped and chopped
1 medium onion, chopped
3 cloves garlic, crushed
1 medium red pepper, seeded and diced
60 ml (4 tbsp) tomato purée (see p. 208)
6 pita breads
thinly sliced Mozzarella cheese
dried origanum
olive oil

Sauté mushrooms, onion, garlic and red pepper in the minimum amount of oil until softened and all the liquid has evaporated. Tip into a bowl and stir in the tomato purée – set aside at this stage if you are working ahead. Spread the mixture over the tops of the pitas, cover with cheese, sprinkle with origanum and drizzle a little olive oil over each. Place on a large baking tray and bake at 200 °C (400 °F, Gas Mark 6) for 15–20 minutes until cheese has melted and the pitas are piping hot.

TOMATO AND CHEDDAR TOPPING
Simply spread each pita with a little tomato purée (not tomato sauce), then cover with fresh, thinly sliced tomatoes, a pinch of salt, crushed garlic, chopped spring onions, a sprinkling of herbs (fresh or dried), a drizzle of olive oil, plenty of grated Cheddar cheese, and finally some milled black pepper. Place on a baking tray and bake at 200 °C (400 °F, Gas Mark 6) for about 20 minutes, or position the tray towards the bottom of the oven and grill until the cheese has melted.
MAKES 24 WEDGES.

Roasted Vegetables in Phyllo Baskets

Everything about this starter caters to fashion: roasted **vegetables, phyllo pastry, yoghurt** – they're all high on the list of popular foods. Preparation requires three steps; these are not quick, but they're also *not complicated*, and everything can be done in advance.

PHYLLO BASKETS

Buy frozen phyllo pastry and follow the packet instructions for thawing before use. When ready, lay the pastry flat on a dry kitchen towel, cover with another dry towel, and then with a damp one, and keep it like this, uncovering only when needed. Have some oil or an oil/butter mixture ready, for example 15 ml (1 tbsp) butter melted in 45 ml (3 tbsp) oil. Oil large muffin tins and cut squares of phyllo to fit, with a 3 cm (1¼ in) overlap. Let the overlap stand up around the rims – it will look ragged, but this is correct. Brush one square with the oil (brush very lightly as excess oil will drip off the edges and onto the floor of the oven), press into the tin, then press in a second oiled square. Continue making the required number of baskets in this way, then bake at 200 °C (400 °F, Gas Mark 6) for about seven minutes until golden brown. Lift out, cool on a rack, then neaten the edges with a pair of kitchen scissors. The baskets may now be stored in an airtight container. If necessary, re-crisp before use at 160 °C (325 °F, Gas Mark 3) for two to three minutes.

ROASTED VEGETABLES
FOR 6–8 BASKETS

300 g (11 oz) brinjals, cubed
    and dégorged
250 g (9 oz) baby marrows,
    pared, halved and sliced
    (prepared weight)
1 medium red pepper, seeded
    and diced
2 medium leeks (white parts only),
    thinly sliced
125 g (4½ oz) white mushrooms,
    wiped and halved
3 large sprigs rosemary

DRESSING
60 ml (4 tbsp) olive oil
2 cloves garlic, crushed
10 ml (2 tsp) honey
a little salt

Mix all the vegetables in a large baking dish, tuck in rosemary, toss with mixed dressing and bake at 200 °C (400 °F, Gas Mark 6) for 15 minutes. Toss to mix, bake for a further 10 minutes, then turn on oven grill and allow to brown lightly. Leave to cool, tossing once or twice – the vegetables should be tender and glossy. Discard rosemary stems, but return most of the leaves.

To serve, place phyllo baskets on individual plates, fill with vegetables and serve as they are or with Greek or Bulgarian yoghurt flavoured with snipped basil and chives.

SERVES 6–8.

soups

One reason I don't like barbecues is that you don't have **soup** as a first course. The other reason is that I don't like them at all. Invariably it's the same scene: the weather turns funny but the coals are lit and there's no turning back because there's no other food but raw sausage, raw chops, raw everything, so everyone stands around waiting, beer in hand, smoke in eyes, wind in hair, with a wife telling her husband to hurry up because everyone's getting tiddly and he tells her to belt up because he knows what he's doing. It's very difficult for a hostess (who might well have a diploma of sorts under her belt) to hand over the evening's catering to a man who not only is wearing an apron that reads 'You May Quiche The Cook', but who (and she knows this because she's had to clean it afterwards) can't even make toast in a toaster. And now suddenly he wants to feed a dozen guests, and there's no pretty tablecloth, no gleaming silver, no candles – and no soup.

The thing about soup is that it softens people up. Gets them in the mood. They start anticipating. Talking to their neighbours. Sipping sherry. Soup also lays a **foundation** – if it's good, the hostess can relax a bit. Everything will have got off to a happy start – and hopefully that's what the following recipes will help to provide.

Once upon a time, long long ago, the soup course could involve the cook in a marathon session with her stock pot and her bones, perhaps a sheep's head or two, a medley of vegetables, bunches of herbs and a bucket or so of water. But times have changed, and so has the workplace. These days many cooks go to the office, and when they get home, they don't switch on the stove and take out a soup kettle, they switch on the television set and take off their shoes. And so none of these recipes takes a day in the making. They don't contain anything alarming like sops or trotters, and there's a choice of both hot or cold. Choose one to fit the mood, and the season.

soups

Spiced Butternut Soup with Coconut

I am told that the 'proper' name for **butternut squash** is *Caryoka nuciferum*, which makes for a lovely title if you can get your tongue round it: Spiced Caryoka Nuciferum Soup with **Coconut**. What it boils down to, though, is simply a delicious new version of an old favourite.

250 ml (9 fl oz) milk

125 ml (40 g/1½ oz) desiccated coconut (preferably fine)

30 ml (2 tbsp) oil

15 ml (1 tbsp) butter

2 large onions, chopped

7 ml (1½ tsp) curry powder

7 ml (1½ tsp) ground cumin

15 ml (1 tbsp) peeled, chopped root ginger

500 g (1 lb 2 oz) butternut, peeled and cubed (prepared weight)

2 medium sweet apples, peeled and chopped

1 large potato, peeled and cubed

1 litre (1¾ pints) chicken or vegetable stock

2 ml (½ tsp) paprika

1 fat stick cinnamon

a little salt

fresh coriander leaves to garnish

Slowly bring the milk and coconut to the boil, then set aside to cool. Heat the oil and butter, add the onions and, when softening, add the curry powder, cumin and ginger. Toss briefly, then mix in the butternut, apples and potato. Add the remaining ingredients, cover and simmer over a low heat until the vegetables are soft, about 25 minutes. Cool for a while, discard the cinnamon stick, then purée in a blender until smooth. Pour the coconut-milk mixture through a fine mesh sieve – use the back of a spoon to extract all the liquid – you should have 200 ml (7 fl oz). Discard the coconut. Gently reheat the soup, stir in the coconut-milk and heat, stirring, just to boiling point. Check seasoning, pour into small, heated soup bowls and float one or two coriander leaves on top.

SERVES 6.

Low-fat Cream of Carrot Soup

If you're looking for a sensible, **healthy starter** which doesn't appear lean or mean, here it is. Although it's much lower in kilojoules than your average cream of something soup, this one is surprisingly good – **smooth** in texture, **bright** in colour, **spicy** in flavour. Another bonus: it's downright cheap.

1 large onion, chopped

400 g (14 oz) carrots, scraped
and chopped

1 large potato, peeled and cubed

1 sweet apple, peeled and cubed

10 ml (2 tsp) peeled, chopped
root ginger

5 ml (1 tsp) ground cumin

1 stick cinnamon

1 ml (¼ tsp) paprika

3 bay leaves

1.25 litres (2¼ pints) chicken
or vegetable stock

a little salt and a pinch of sugar

90 ml (6 tbsp) instant, fat-free
milk powder

125 ml (4½ fl oz) water

lemon juice

to garnish? Easy. A fat-free herb
or flower.

Combine everything except the milk powder, water and lemon juice in a large saucepan. Bring to the boil, then cover and simmer until the vegetables are soft. Leave to cool. Discard the cinnamon and bay leaves, then purée in a blender. You will have to do this in two or three batches – if the mixture is too thick to blend smoothly, add a little extra stock. Return to the saucepan. Stir the milk powder into the water, add it to the soup and reheat gently, stirring. Check seasoning – it will probably need a little more salt, an extra pinch of sugar, and a dash of lemon juice to bring out the flavour. Serve hot.
SERVES 4–6.

* Sometimes I add an extra spoon of milk powder for an even creamier texture, and sometimes I add a small handful of fresh coriander leaves when reheating – it makes it doubly delicious.

31

Smoked Salmon Vichyssoise

Simply scrumptious. Although **smoked salmon** is the quintessential ingredient, only a modest amount is required to tart up a basic **vichyssoise**. The result is a soup that makes men propose.

15 ml (1 tbsp) oil
15 ml (1 tbsp) butter
2 large leeks, sliced
1 medium onion, chopped
400 g (14 oz) potatoes, peeled
  and diced
2 ml (½ tsp) paprika
1 litre (1¾ pints) fish stock
2 ml (½ tsp) finely grated
  lemon rind
120 g (4 oz) smoked salmon slices
  (thawed if frozen), chopped
125 ml (4½ fl oz) cream
15 ml (1 tbsp) medium-dry sherry
lemon juice and/or a few drops
  of Tabasco
a nicked slice of lemon on the
  rim of each bowl, or a frond of
  dill to garnish, nothing elaborate

Heat the oil and butter and soften the leeks and onions without browning – this is best achieved by covering the saucepan and letting them sweat over very low heat. Add the potatoes and paprika and toss to mix, then add the stock and lemon rind. Bring to the boil, then cover and simmer gently until the potatoes are soft. Add the salmon, stir to heat through, then remove from heat and cool until 'blender-friendly' (warm, not hot). Purée until smooth. Return to the saucepan and, when just popping, stir in the cream (you might need a little more cream or even a dash of milk if the soup is too thick). Add the sherry and stir until piping hot, but do not let it boil. Check seasoning, highlight the flavour with just a dash of lemon juice and/or Tabasco to taste, and pour into heated bowls. Serve with melba toast and pass a pepper mill.

SERVES 5–6.

Mushroom, Leek and Whiskey Soup

I once spent a night in a telephone booth. I think it was in Sneem. Or was it Inch? Then again, it could have been Killybegs. Anyway, it was somewhere in Ireland. I had hitched a lift (you could in those days) and was dumped rather unexpectedly in the wee hours when my driver decided to change his route. The only light in the village came from a telephone booth, so I stepped inside and stayed there with my bags until the postman found me in the morning and took me to a kind landlady just up the road. She didn't ask any questions, she simply put on her apron. 'For sure,' she clucked, 'ye'd be needing a plate o' Bushmills.' This turned out to be a dish of oats porridge with a shot of whiskey poured round, drizzled with *honey* and *yellow cream*. The Irish do such lovely things with their whiskey...

250 g (9 oz) white mushrooms
15 ml (1 tbsp) each oil and butter
3 slim leeks, finely shredded
1 medium onion, finely chopped
1 ml (¼ tsp) grated nutmeg
2 ml (½ tsp) finely grated
  lemon rind
30 ml (2 tbsp) whiskey
30 ml (2 tbsp) flour
600 ml (1 pint) hot chicken stock
a little salt
2 ml (½ tsp) soft brown sugar
60 ml (4 tbsp) cream
15 ml (1 tbsp) extra whiskey

Set aside two mushroom caps, then wipe and chop the remainder. Heat the oil and butter, add the onion and leeks and sweat until soft and translucent. Add the chopped mushrooms, nutmeg and lemon rind, toss for a minute over low heat, then add the 30 ml (2 tbsp) whiskey and cook until evaporated.

Sprinkle in the flour and when absorbed slowly stir in the stock, salt and sugar. Cover and simmer gently for 10 minutes. Leave to cool, then purée briefly in a blender – the mixture should be slightly chunky. Return to the saucepan, add the cream and extra whiskey and stir until piping hot. Check seasoning, pour into small, heated bowls and garnish each serving with the reserved (uncooked) mushrooms, wiped and slivered.

SERVES 4–5.

Chilled Celery Soup with Smoked Salmon and Cucumber Cups

It's the salmon that makes this basic *cream soup* so special. Combined with crisp *cucumber*, the mixture is set in small coffee cups, then unmoulded and surrounded with the *delicately flavoured* soup. The unusual presentation and contrast in textures make this a *stunning*, special-occasion starter.

SMOKED SALMON CUPS

125 g (4½ oz) smoked salmon
   off-cuts, finely chopped
250 ml (125 g/4½ oz) finely
   diced, pared, deseeded
   English cucumber (patted dry)
10 ml (2 tsp) lemon juice
2–3 spring onions, chopped
5 ml (1 tsp) gelatine dissolved
   in 60 ml (4 tbsp) chicken or
   vegetable stock

SOUP

30 ml (2 tbsp) oil
10 ml (2 tsp) butter
1 large onion, chopped
½ large English cucumber,
   pared, seeded and diced
3 large sticks table celery,
   plus leaves, chopped
1 fairly large potato, peeled
   and cubed
5 ml (1 tsp) dried dill
1 litre (1¾ pints) chicken or
   vegetable stock
2 bay leaves
a few sprigs of parsley
salt to taste and a pinch of sugar
250 ml (9 fl oz) milk

cultured sour cream and milled
   black pepper to garnish

Mix the salmon, cucumber, lemon juice and onions, stir in the gelatine and spoon into six rinsed little cups. Cover and refrigerate. To make the soup, heat the oil and butter, add the onion, cucumber, celery, potato and dill, toss to mix, then cover and sweat over low heat for a few minutes – the vegetables should soften without browning. Add the remaining ingredients, except the milk, then cover and simmer gently for about 25 minutes until the vegetables are soft. Cool until no longer steaming, discard the bay leaves, add the milk and purée in a blender until smooth. Check seasoning, pour into a fridge container, cover and refrigerate. To serve, unmould the salmon cups into the centre of each soup plate and pour the soup around. Top each mould with sour cream and dust with milled black pepper.
SERVES 6.

Lebanese Soup

An intriguing, sunny-coloured soup, with **spices** adding character and an **exotic flavour** to a basic **cauliflower** purée.

30 ml (2 tbsp) oil
15 ml (1 tbsp) butter
1 large onion, chopped
2 cloves garlic, crushed
5 ml (1 tsp) ground cumin
2 ml (½ tsp) turmeric
400–500 g (14 oz–1 lb 2 oz)
   cauliflower florets
1 litre (1¾ pints) hot chicken
   or vegetable stock
2 bay leaves
125 ml (90 g/3¼ oz) red lentils,
   rinsed
2 ml (½ tsp) chilli powder
a little salt and a pinch of sugar
about 250 ml (9 fl oz) milk
a little fresh lemon juice
fresh coriander leaves or snipped
   chives to garnish

Heat the oil and butter in a large saucepan, add the onion and garlic and soften without browning. Add the cumin and turmeric and toss over low heat to release the flavours, then add the cauliflower and toss until coated. Add the remaining ingredients, except the milk and lemon juice, and bring to the boil. Reduce heat and simmer, covered, for about 20 minutes, stirring once, until the cauliflower is mushy and the lentils have disintegrated. Allow to cool for a while, discard the bay leaves, then purée in a blender until smooth – do this in two or three batches. If working ahead, turn into a bowl and refrigerate. Reheat gently with enough milk to achieve the desired consistency. Check seasoning and add a dash of lemon juice to highlight the flavour.
SERVES 6.

Dilled Baby Marrow and Celery Soup

Baby marrows are such eager-to-please little vegetables, so willing and so happy to pitch in with any other ingredient, that I really find them very endearing. This soup is just one example – instead of arguing with the other vegetables, like a parsnip would, they simply melt in and perfect the flavour. This is a simple and reliable soup which can be served hot or cold.

30 ml (2 tbsp) oil
15 ml (1 tbsp) butter
2 medium leeks, chopped
1 small onion, chopped
300 g (11 oz) baby marrows, trimmed, pared and sliced (prepared weight)
2 sticks table celery, plus some leaves, chopped
1 large potato, peeled and cubed
5 ml (1 tsp) dried dill
1 litre (1¾ pints) chicken or vegetable stock
3 bay leaves
a few sprigs of parsley
a little salt and a pinch of sugar
300 ml (11 fl oz) milk
lemon juice
cream and fresh dill to garnish

Heat the butter and oil in a large saucepan, add the leeks and onion, cover and sweat over low heat until softened. Add the marrows, celery, potato and dill and toss for a few minutes – keep the heat low as nothing should start to brown. Add the remaining ingredients, except the milk and lemon juice, and cover and simmer for about 25 minutes until the vegetables are very soft. Cool, discard the bay leaves, add the milk and purée in batches in a blender – for the best texture do this in several batches until the mixture is a pale lemon colour, flecked with green. Check seasoning, sharpen with a little lemon juice if you think it needs it, and either reheat gently, or chill very well – up to 24 hours. To finish off, softly whip about 125 ml (4½ fl oz) cream and fold in 10 ml (2 tsp) chopped fresh dill leaves. Swirl a spoonful into each bowl of soup.

SERVES 6–8.

Easy Mushroom Bouillon

This is a **quick-to-make**, thin soup with a lovely balance of **oriental flavours**. Sophisticated and low in kilojoules, it makes an excellent starter to whet appetites before a fine dinner. And it reheats well.

1½ litres (2¾ pints) chicken stock

3 stalks of lemon grass (fleshy white part, bruised, outer layer removed), chopped

1 star anise

a chunk of root ginger, peeled and coarsely grated – about 15 ml (1 tbsp)

a few tufts of parsley

a pinch of sugar

5 ml (1 tsp) sesame oil

45 ml (3 tbsp) medium-dry sherry

30 ml (2 tbsp) soy sauce

125 g (4½ oz) white mushrooms, wiped and sliced

3–4 spring onions, finely chopped

iced carrot strips to garnish (shave a carrot thinly, drop the slivers into iced water, refrigerate and drain before using)

Put all the ingredients, except the mushrooms and onions, into a saucepan. Slowly bring to the boil, then reduce heat, cover and simmer for 20 minutes – you should become aware of a bewitching, gingery-lemon aroma. Cool completely to allow the flavours to mellow, then strain. Just before dinner, reheat to boiling, add the mushrooms and onions and simmer, half-covered, for 10 minutes. Check seasoning and serve in small bowls. Sprinkle with the garnish, and, if liked, serve with sesame toasts: cream 125 g (4½ oz) butter with 30 ml (2 tbsp) toasted sesame seeds and two chopped spring onions. Toast the fingers of bread on one side, spread untoasted side with the butter mixture, and grill.

SOUP SERVES 4–6.

Stephen's Soup

As a child my son often asked for – and got – **soup** for breakfast. As a result I can now make thick and hearty soups in my sleep. This quick version, also known as Thirty-minute **Minestrone**, is a chunky meal-in-a-bowl which will satisfy the sharpest appetite, morning, noon or night.

30 ml (2 tbsp) olive oil
2 medium onions, finely chopped
3 cloves garlic, crushed
5 ml (1 tsp) mixed dried herbs
   or Italian herbs
500 g (1 lb 2 oz) mixed frozen
   vegetables*
1 x 410 g (14 oz) can tomatoes,
   chopped, plus juice
60 ml (4 tbsp) red wine
5 ml (1 tsp) salt
10 ml (2 tsp) sugar
1 litre (1¾ pints) chicken or
   vegetable stock
a handful of chopped parsley
125 ml (60 g/2 oz) anellini, or other
   small pasta noodles
1 x 410 g (14 oz) can baked beans
   in tomato sauce
basil pesto and/or grated
   Parmesan cheese for serving

Heat the oil in a large, heavy saucepan and sauté the onions and garlic. Add the dried herbs and toss to mix, then add the frozen vegetables, tomatoes, wine, seasoning, stock and parsley. Bring to the boil, add the pasta, then cover and simmer for 10 minutes, stirring once or twice. Add the baked beans and simmer gently for a further 10 minutes. Check seasoning, and add extra stock if necessary, but remember that this hearty soup should be thick. Serve in deep soup plates, with a teaspoon of pesto swirled into each, and pass round a bowl of Parmesan and a loaf of floury ciabatta.

SERVES 6.

* Use finely chopped, choice vegetables such as beans, carrots, cauliflower, peas, and preferably including corn.

Pumpkin Soup with Mascarpone

Spiked with **orange**, fresh **ginger** and **cinnamon**, and enriched with melting **mascarpone cheese**, this soup is simply one of the best. Mascarpone, made from **fresh cream**, is a sweet, rich cheese usually reserved for desserts – but it harmonises perfectly with the flavours in this soup and adds a silky touch of luxury.

30 ml (2 tbsp) oil
15 ml (1 tbsp) butter
1 large onion, chopped
30 ml (2 tbsp) peeled, roughly
   chopped root ginger
500 g (1 lb 2 oz) bright orange
   pumpkin, peeled and cubed
   (prepared weight)
1 medium carrot, diced
1 fairly large potato, peeled
   and diced
grated rind of 1 medium orange
2 ml (½ tsp) paprika
1 litre (1¾ pints) hot chicken or
   vegetable stock
2 sticks cinnamon
a little salt and a large pinch
   of sugar
mascarpone cheese
snipped chives to garnish

Heat the oil and butter, add the onion and ginger and allow to soften without browning. Add the pumpkin (be sure to remove all the peel – there should not be a trace of green on the flesh), together with the carrot, potato, orange rind and paprika. Toss until coated and aromatic, then add the remaining ingredients, except the cheese. Cover and simmer gently for about 20 minutes until the vegetables are soft. Set aside until absolutely cool to allow the flavours to infuse. Discard the cinnamon and purée in a blender until smooth, adding a little extra stock if too thick. Return the mixture to the saucepan, then add the mascarpone – start with 60 g (2 oz), which will be enough for some tastes, but increase it for a creamier, richer soup. Stir over a low heat until very hot, then pour into small heated bowls. Top each serving with a flutter of chives.

SERVES 6.

Chunky Tomato and Shrimp Soup

This is not a fancy fish soup, it's really very basic and very simple: a little **pasta**, a couple of **shrimps**, lots of fresh **vegetables** and just right for supper with garlic bread, red wine and a fire.

30 ml (2 tbsp) olive oil

15 ml (1 tbsp) butter

1 large onion, chopped

2 medium carrots, finely diced

2 sticks table celery, plus some
   leaves, finely chopped

a pinch of dried thyme

750 g (1¾ lb) ripe tomatoes, skinned
   and finely chopped (not canned)

1 litre (1¾ pints) hot chicken stock

2 cloves garlic, crushed

2 bay leaves

125 ml (4½ fl oz) tomato purée
   (see p. 208)

a little salt

10 ml (2 tsp) sugar

60 ml (4 tbsp) conchigliette, or
   other very small pasta shapes

1 x 300 g (11 oz) packet frozen,
   cleaned, peeled, uncooked shrimps

a few drops of Tabasco (optional)

fresh basil to garnish

Heat the oil and butter in a large saucepan, add the onion, carrots and celery and sweat very gently until softened, shaking the pan occasionally. Don't hurry this step, it should take at least 10 minutes. Add the thyme towards the end. Add the remaining ingredients, except the pasta, shrimps and Tabasco, bring to the boil, then reduce heat, cover and simmer over low heat – it should just pop gently – for about 25 minutes. Stir once or twice to 'melt' the tomatoes into the broth. Discard the bay leaves, add the pasta, and simmer for 5 minutes. Meanwhile rinse the shrimps under running cold water. Add them to the soup, return to the boil and simmer for a further 5 minutes or until cooked. Check seasoning, spike with Tabasco if using, ladle into heated bowls and garnish.

SERVES 6–8.

* It is important that all the vegetables be chopped into small pieces as the soup is meant to be chunky, not crunchy.

Minted Cream of Celery and Cucumber Soup

Adding a potato to the vegetables is quite the best way of thickening these velvety soups without masking the flavour, and this pale and interesting beauty is a good example. **Hot or cold**, it is good both ways.

30 ml (2 tbsp) oil

10 ml (2 tsp) butter

1 large onion, chopped

½ large English cucumber, pared and diced

1 medium potato, peeled and cubed

2 large sticks table celery, plus some leaves, chopped

750 ml (1¼ pints) chicken or vegetable stock

2 bay leaves

a few sprigs of parsley

a large pinch each of salt and sugar

250 ml (9 fl oz) milk

about 12 mint leaves, chopped or 5 ml (1 tsp) dried dill

fresh mint, fresh dill, or julienned cucumber to garnish

Heat the oil and butter in a large saucepan and add the onion, cucumber, potato and celery. If using dill instead of mint, add it with the vegetables. Cover and sweat over low heat for a few minutes, shaking the pan occasionally to prevent catching – do not allow to brown. Add the stock, bay leaves, parsley and seasoning. Cover and simmer until all the vegetables are soft – the heat should be kept very low in order to retain all the stock. Cool until the mixture stops steaming, then add the milk and mint leaves if using. Purée in batches in a blender until smooth – the mixture should be medium-thick and flecked with mint or dill. It may be sieved for ultra-smoothness, if you feel up to it. If serving hot, reheat in a saucepan rinsed with cold water or in a double-boiler. If serving cold, chill very well. Garnish before serving.

SERVES 6 if you use small bowls, rather than soup plates.

starter salads

I once saw a waiter carrying a large **green salad** to a table. I was a dining-out columnist at the time and was doing a write-up on this particular restaurant. I'd just settled down with the menu and a glass of wine when this waiter passed me – carrying a large green salad to a table. What made this otherwise ordinary sight extraordinary was the fact that as he passed a pillar, he suddenly stopped, stepped behind it, and thrust the **serving fork** inside his sleeve and up his arm. He was wearing one of those balloony silky blouse-shirts, like the English kings used to pose in for their portraits. Well, he thrust the fork up his sleeve where there's a slit in the cuff and had a good long scratch – up, down, and around. Then he whipped it out, put it back in the **bowl**, stepped from behind the pillar, and placed the green salad on the table. Now, as a food writer, one has some ticklish experiences, but this was one of my worst. I was in an awful dilemma. Should I tell the diners at that table where their fork had just been? I mean, wasn't it my duty? What if they all came out in rashes and it was my fault for not telling? And what if I did tell and they told the manager and the waiter was fired? His poor old mother. He was definitely supporting a poor old mother. So what did I do? I sipped my **wine** and thought for a long time. Mum's the word, I finally decided. I then put my notebook away, scotched the review, attacked the menu, and had a lovely evening.

Starter salads have, to a large extent, replaced the fishy mousses and layered terrines we used to slave over just a few years ago. This makes good sense to me, as a starter salad lends itself to some innovative creations which rarely take long to prepare, and they don't fill you up too much, which means the main course will be fully appreciated. The salad recipes in this section are for this type of salad, rather than the leafy side-dish variety.

starter salads

Green Salad with Blue Cheese Dressing

A mixture of **greens**, **nuts** and **croûtons** responds really well to the flavour of **blue cheese**, and the following combination makes a jumbo salad starter. Prepare the greens and dressing in advance and toss just before serving. Because it is such a flexible mixture and there's plenty of dressing, you can add extra leafy things to the salad if you wish to pad it even further.

1 very large bunch of spinach
1 butter lettuce, or other loose-
  leaved lettuce (not iceberg)
400 g (14 oz) broccoli
walnuts or pecan nuts, preferably
  lightly roasted, coarsely
  chopped, and/or croûtons
mixed sprouts to garnish

DRESSING
250 ml (9 fl oz) oil, at least half
  olive oil
90 ml (6 tbsp) lemon juice
90 g (3¼ oz) blue cheese, cubed
  (or more to taste)
5 ml (1 tsp) Worcestershire sauce
1 small clove garlic, chopped
a few tufts of parsley
2 spring onions, chopped
5 ml (1 tsp) sugar

Remove the ribs from the washed, dried spinach. Roll the leaves into wads and use a sharp knife to shred thinly. Tear the lettuce into small pieces. Steam the broccoli just until crisp-tender, then chop. Mix all the vegetables in a large bowl and add the nuts. Place all the ingredients for the dressing in a blender goblet and blend until creamy. Just before serving, toss the greens with a spoon of oil – this allows the dressing to adhere better – then toss with the dressing. Mix in the croûtons if using, and garnish.

SERVES 10.

Grilled Nutty Feta on Salad Leaves with Rosemary and Lemon Dressing

A starter of green salad topped with warm, grilled cheese has become very fashionable and is so easy to prepare that it hardly merits a recipe. This version, however, gives plain grilled cheese a delicious and unusual lift with a pesto-almond topping. Goat's cheese is the one most recipes suggest, but feta is my personal preference and is always available. The salad dressing – a thick and creamy blend of herbs and lemon – is one to treasure, and will transform any green salad as well, so I have supplied a generous recipe. Here it perfectly complements the combination of hot, nutty cheese and crisp salad leaves.

ROSEMARY AND LEMON SALAD DRESSING

3 x 10 cm (4 in) sprigs rosemary
600 ml (1 pint) oil
125 ml (4½ fl oz) lemon juice
10 ml (2 tsp) mustard powder
2–3 cloves garlic, chopped
30 ml (2 tbsp) honey
15 ml (1 tbsp) Balsamic vinegar
grated rind of 1 lemon
a few tufts of parsley
a pinch of salt
60 ml (4 tbsp) water

Strip the leaves from the rosemary sprigs and place in a blender with the remaining ingredients. Blend well until the mixture is pale, creamy and flecked with green. Pour into a glass jar and refrigerate. Shake well before using.

Makes 750 ml (1¼ pints).

SALAD

400 g (14 oz) feta cheese
   (6 rounds)
basil pesto
slivered almonds
a mixture of salad leaves –
   use baby spinach and
   different lettuces

Arrange the rounds of feta on a flat ovenproof plate. Spread each round with 5–10 ml (1–2 tsp) pesto and top with a layer of almonds. Grill until hot and the almonds are lightly browned – be careful here, if you turn your back the nuts will burn – it is best to position the plate well below the grill (set on medium). Toss the salad leaves with just enough of the dressing to gloss, pile onto individual serving plates, top each with a round of the grilled cheese, and serve with hot, herbed pitas or focaccia.

SERVES 6.

Avocado, Mushroom and Pear Salad with Blue Cheese Dressing

There are no half measures with **blue cheese**. People either love it or hate it. The smell either makes them drool, or they start looking round for the wet dog. But if you are a fan, you'll love this salad. Although it's really quick to prepare, the flavours are complex and rich, so it's best served simply with melba toast.

2 medium avocado pears,
  peeled and thinly segmented
125 g (4½ oz) button mushrooms,
  wiped and thinly sliced
2 ripe pears, peeled and thinly
  segmented
45 ml (3 tbsp) lemon juice

DRESSING
125 ml (4½ fl oz) mayonnaise
125 ml (4½ fl oz) thick
  Bulgarian yoghurt
a dash of Worcestershire sauce
about 45 g (1½ oz) blue cheese,
  crumbled*
a pinch of salt
5 ml (1 tsp) honey

milled black pepper and chopped
  walnuts to garnish

Place the avocado, mushrooms and pears in three separate bowls and toss each with 15 ml (1 tbsp) lemon juice, then arrange in layers in one flat serving dish, or divide between six individual bowls. Stir together the ingredients for the dressing until fairly smooth, using more or less cheese, according to taste. Spoon over the salad to cover, then cover and refrigerate for 3–4 hours. Garnish just before serving.
SERVES 6.

* If you don't like blue cheese, flavour the dressing with grainy mustard instead.

Roasted Pepper and Mushroom Salad with Oriental Dressing

This is an unlikely combination, but it works surprisingly well and makes a delectable, unusual first course, served with slices of **French bread** toasted on one side, spread with a **herbed butter** (garlic and lemon, or tarragon and parsley) and grilled until bubbling.

DRESSING
125 ml (4½ fl oz) oil
10 ml (2 tsp) dark sesame oil
30 ml (2 tbsp) toasted
  sesame seeds*
60 ml (4 tbsp) lemon juice
30 ml (2 tbsp) honey
20 ml (4 tsp) soy sauce
2 small cloves garlic, crushed
a few spring onions, chopped

SALAD
2 large red peppers
2 large yellow peppers
250 g (9 oz) white mushrooms,
  wiped and thinly sliced
extra sesame seeds to garnish

Mix all the ingredients for the dressing and set aside. Wash and halve all the peppers, remove seeds and ribs, press to flatten and grill until blackened. Wrap the peppers in a damp cloth for a few minutes, then skin and sliver. Place in a large, shallow salad bowl, add the mushrooms and dressing, toss until well mixed, then cover with cling wrap and refrigerate for 4–6 hours. Stand at room temperature for about 15 minutes before serving. Garnish with a light sprinkling of sesame seeds.

SERVES 6–8.

* Spread a thin layer of seeds over the base of a non-stick frying pan and dry-roast over low heat until golden-brown, shaking the pan occasionally.

Stuffed Tomatoes

8 firm, medium-sized tomatoes

Pour boiling water over the tomatoes, leave for a minute, then rinse under cold running water and remove skins. Slice off the tops, scoop out most of the insides, and leave upside down to drain. Fill just before serving.

SMOKED SALMON FILLING
120 g (4 oz) smoked salmon
   off-cuts, chopped
250 g (9 oz) smooth, low-fat
   cottage cheese (see p. 208)
15 ml (1 tbsp) lemon juice
2 slim spring onions, chopped
45 ml (3 tbsp) soft butter
a pinch of sugar
10 ml (2 tsp) Pernod (optional)

Mash together all the ingredients until very well combined. Refrigerate until just before dinner. Fill prepared tomatoes and dust with milled black pepper.

HERBED RICOTTA FILLING
400 g (14 oz) Ricotta cheese
75–90 ml (5–6 tbsp) cream
2 ml (½ tsp) salt
30 ml (2 tbsp) each chopped
   chives and parsley
8–10 large, fresh basil leaves
a dash of lemon juice

Place all the ingredients in a processor fitted with the metal blade and process until smooth. Spoon into a container and refrigerate for a few hours. Fill the prepared tomatoes and garnish with fresh basil.

SERVES 8.

Spinach and Mushroom Salad with Creamy Parmesan Dressing

Although this salad will perk up many a dish very nicely, it is flawless served with *pasta* sauced with *fresh tomatoes*, or as a robust starter with *warm ciabatta*. Tossing the salad ingredients in *French dressing* first, ensures that the creamy dressing will adhere to the leaves.

2 bunches young spinach OR
   1 bunch spinach and 1 cos lettuce*
250 g (9 oz) white mushrooms,
   wiped and thinly sliced
1 bunch spring onions, chopped
sun-dried tomatoes in oil, drained

DRESSING (1)
60 ml (4 tbsp) oil
45 ml (3 tbsp) lemon juice
2 ml (½ tsp) each dried origanum
   and sugar
a pinch of salt

DRESSING (2)
60 ml (4 tbsp) grated
   Parmesan cheese
60 ml (4 tbsp) mayonnaise
60 ml (4 tbsp) Greek yoghurt
   or cultured sour cream

milled black pepper
chopped walnuts or pecans

Remove the stems and ribs from the spinach, and cos lettuce if using. Wash well, spin dry, roll the leaves up tightly and slice across into thin shreds. You should have about 360 g (12–13 oz). Place the shredded leaves in a large bowl and add the mushrooms and onions. Sliver enough sun-dried tomatoes to provide 60–90 ml (4–6 tbsp) and mix them in. Mix dressing (1), pour over the greens, toss well, then cover securely and stand for 1–2 hours. Meanwhile mix the ingredients for dressing (2) and refrigerate. Just before serving, mix everything together – the creamy dressing is thick, so a good toss is necessary to combine the ingredients thoroughly. Add a few grinds of pepper, and a handful of nuts.

SERVES 8.

* If you can't find young spinach, use organically grown Swiss chard.

Leeks Provençale

Once chopped, **leeks** often disappear into a stew or soup never to be seen again, but in this starter salad they are allowed to retain their individuality and the resulting mingle of **Mediterranean flavours** makes a fitting beginning to a meal of pasta, or a rustic, meaty casserole. Do use **fresh thyme** if possible – in this case no other herb matches up quite as well – and serve with a hot, **garlic-buttered baguette**.

400 g (14 oz) slender leeks
90 ml (6 tbsp) olive oil
90 ml (6 tbsp) water
90 ml (6 tbsp) red wine
3–4 cloves garlic, crushed
12 sprigs fresh thyme and/or
  lemon thyme
4 bay leaves
5 ml (1 tsp) salt
10 ml (2 tsp) sugar
400 g (14 oz) tomatoes, chopped
  (not skinned)
20–24 black olives
chopped parsley to garnish

Trim the roots, outer leaves and green tops from the leeks, then slice into 2 cm (¾ in) chunks and wash well. Put into a large frying pan with the remaining ingredients, except the tomatoes and black olives. Bring to the boil, then reduce the heat and simmer, covered, for 5 minutes. Gently mix in the tomatoes and simmer for a further 5 minutes, until the mixture is soft, but not mushy. Add the olives and heat through if serving hot, or turn into a large, shallow bowl and cool. Remove the thyme and bay leaves and garnish with parsley just before serving.
SERVES 8.

Low-oil Dressing

For those cutting kilojoules in their dressings, here's a surprisingly pleasant splosh for **green salads**, with none of that strident vinegary flavour.

250 ml (9 fl oz) water
10 ml (2 tsp) cornflour
5 ml (1 tsp) mustard powder
2 ml (½ tsp) paprika
30 ml (2 tbsp) lemon juice
5 ml (1 tsp) balsamic vinegar
60 ml (4 tbsp) oil
1 clove garlic, crushed
a pinch of salt
10 ml (2 tsp) honey

Mix the water, cornflour, mustard powder, paprika, lemon juice, vinegar, oil, garlic and a pinch of salt in a deep saucepan, then bring it to the boil, stirring. Let the mixture bubble rapidly for a minute, then remove from heat and add the honey. Cool, bottle and refrigerate – it keeps for up to three days. Stir before using.

MAKES 325 ML (11 FL OZ)

Best Greek Salad

I've said it before and I'm going to say it again: Why are there no *brinjals* in Greek salads? Almost every restaurant features a Greek salad, and almost every restaurant serves up the same pedestrian pile  of raw onions, tomato, cucumber, lettuce, raw onions, feta, olives and raw onions. It might be the *traditional Salata*, but it's boring. In fact, it's a Greek tragedy – when you think of all the lovely *Mediterranean vegetables* one could include. This 'Greek' salad takes just a little more time to prepare, but it's visually stunning, and if you serve it with interesting *breads* and preface it with *soup*, it makes a complete meal. It's also good as a starter, or with roast lamb.

Best Greek Salad

1 x 300 g (11 oz) brinjal, cubed,
   dégorged, rinsed and dried
6 cloves garlic, unpeeled
1–2 red peppers, halved,
   seeded and flattened
lots of salad leaves*, including
   shredded spinach
4 tomatoes, diced
1 Spanish onion, sliced into rings**
a handful of fresh basil leaves, torn
a few sun-dried tomatoes,
   drained and slivered
about 250 g (9 oz) feta cheese,
   diced
black olives

DRESSING
250 ml (9 fl oz) olive oil
15 ml (1 tbsp) Balsamic vinegar
30 ml (2 tbsp) lemon juice
15 ml (1 tbsp) honey
2 ml (½ tsp) mustard powder

64

Place the prepared brinjal cubes and garlic in a bowl and toss with 15 ml (1 tbsp) olive oil. Spread out, with the peppers, on a baking tray (lined with baking paper if you wish) or in a flat, shallow baking dish, and roast at 200 °C (400 °F, Gas Mark 6) until tender. Drain on paper towels, then tip the brinjals into a big bowl, snip off the tips of the garlic and squeeze the flesh onto the brinjals, tossing to mix. Dice the red pepper and add it to the brinjal-garlic mixture, together with the salad leaves, tomatoes, onion and basil – you could toss in some cucumber too if you like. Spoon the whole lot onto a large platter and garnish with the sun-dried tomatoes, feta and olives. Whizz the ingredients for the dressing in a blender, and serve separately.

SERVES 8–10.

* No accurate weight can be given for leaves as this depends on the varieties used, but you should have eight large cupfuls, or enough to fill a 2 litre (3½ pint) jug.
** You may wonder what a Spanish onion is doing in a Greek salad – but never mind – the flavour of these sweet, red-skinned onions is a universal treat. If unobtainable, substitute chopped spring onions.

fish

Anyone brought up in the Karoo will understand my fear of **fish**. As a child, I never got to seeing a proper fish because there aren't any in the Karoo. Frogs and lizards and snakes in abundance, but no proper fish. It's a dry place, this Karoo, and it's far from the **sea** and the rivers are usually empty of everything, including water. The only fish I ever met in the small town in which I spent my childhood, came **crisply battered** and **fried** from the fish shop next to the Post Office. I think it was owned by a Greek because I remember the sign above the door was spelt with strange letters, like á and fth and óu, and his fish was quite the best I have ever eaten. We had it for supper once a week with **chips and vinegar**.

If I hadn't eventually grown up and gone to live in a city by the sea, I would have been contented with fried fish forever. But in the city I had to learn new things, like shopping at supermarkets, and hosting dinner parties, and putting whole **baked fish** with **tartare sauce** on the menu instead of always serving Karoo lamb chops, so I married a fisherman. Or at least a man who liked to fish. He took me out fishing in a boat on a lagoon near Knysna, and as luck would have it I caught a fish first throw. It was a beautiful **Grunter**, and it just lay there sadly on the bottom of the boat and grunted and grunted – and that was the end of it for me. From then on I bought only dead fish without heads and eyes and vocal chords.

I still have a problem with **mussels**. The experts suggest that, to test a raw mussel for freshness, you should tap it with a knife and it should snap shut immediately. One day I was doing this gently, going knock-knock, knock-knock, and I swear I heard a small voice saying 'Who's there?' Now could I drop this voice into a pot? Could you? Never. However, there are other fish in the sea, so to speak, and I've dealt with some in this chapter. Please know that not a single one was caught by me, gutted by me, deheaded or scaled or filleted by me. When you fear fish you leave all that stuff to your brave, friendly **fishmonger**.

PS Other experts say if a mussel is even slightly open, throw it away. So there it is. Or there it went.

fish

Garlicky Hake with Nutty Crumb Topping

 **Hake** should never be regarded as a Cinderella fish.

In certain recipes, such as the following, it is quite the

best choice – not too firm, not too thick and, by

using large, unsliced fillets, this dish is really easy to present

attractively. The *coriander-tzatziki* rounds it off perfectly.

2 large pieces fresh, skinned
   and filleted hake (800–900 g/
   1¾–2 lb in total) (see p. 208)
salt and pepper to season
fresh lemon juice

COATING MIXTURE
45 ml (3 tbsp) butter
45 ml (3 tbsp) olive oil
3 plump cloves garlic, crushed
2 ml (½ tsp) dried tarragon or dill,
   crushed

CRUMB MIXTURE
150 ml (45 g/1½ oz) fine white
   breadcrumbs
125 ml (45 g/1½ oz) finely
   chopped pecan nuts
60 ml (4 tbsp) finely chopped
   parsley
2 ml (½ tsp) finely grated
   lemon rind
a pinch of salt

Melt together all the ingredients for the coating mixture and brush it over the top of the hake. Place buttered side down in a large, shallow baking dish – the fish must lie flat – then brush the other side, reserving the remainder. Season the fish and sprinkle lightly with lemon juice. Mix all the ingredients for the crumb topping, moisten with the reserved coating mixture and sprinkle evenly over the fish. If space allows, surround with halved tomatoes, seasoned and sprinkled with herbs and a little olive oil. Bake, uncovered, at 180 ˚C (350 ˚F, Gas Mark 4) for 25–30 minutes until the topping is toasty-brown and the fish is just cooked through. Carefully transfer the fish and tomatoes to a large, flat and heated serving platter.

TZATZIKI

Sprinkle 250 ml (125 g/4½ oz) pared and diced English cucumber with salt, stand for about 30 minutes, rinse and pat dry (dégorging the cucumber mellows the flavour). Fold the cucumber into 250 ml (9 fl oz) thick and creamy Greek-style yoghurt (or plain, low-fat Bulgarian yoghurt), adding 60 ml (4 tbsp) fresh coriander leaves. Alternatively, omit the cucumber and simply mix 125 ml (4½ fl oz) each Greek yoghurt and Bulgarian yoghurt with the coriander.

SERVES 4–6.

Fish in Tomato and Basil Cream Sauce

Nestled in a bountiful sauce, this fish dish is a bright fanfare of Italian flavours – **tomatoes**, **basil**, **Parmesan**, a touch of **wine** – with a ladle of **cream** sneaked in. For maximum effect, serve with ribbon **noodles** and a leafy **salad** lightly glossed with **Balsamic vinegar** and **olive oil**.

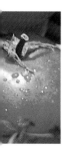

800 g (1¾ lb) skinned white
  fish fillets
olive oil
salt and pepper to season
1 medium onion, finely chopped
2 cloves garlic, crushed
1 x 410 g (14 oz) can tomatoes,
  chopped, plus juice
a little salt
7 ml (1½ tsp) sugar
10 ml (2 tsp) tomato paste
  (see p. 208)
60 ml (4 tbsp) white wine
30 ml (2 tbsp) chopped parsley
60 ml (4 tbsp) chopped fresh
  basil leaves
125 ml (4½ fl oz) cream
10 ml (2 tsp) cornflour
grated Parmesan cheese for topping

Brush the fillets lightly with oil, place in a baking dish, season and bake at 180 °C (350 °F, Gas Mark 4) until just cooked.* Meanwhile make the sauce: heat an extra 30 ml (2 tbsp) olive oil in a frying pan, lightly sauté the onion and garlic, add the tomatoes, salt, sugar, tomato paste, wine and parsley, then cover and simmer over very low heat for 20 minutes, stirring occasionally. Remove from heat, then add the basil, cream and cornflour and purée in a blender. Pour over the fish, sprinkle with cheese and return to the oven until bubbling and the cheese has melted.

SERVES 4–5.

* The initial baking time will vary according to the thickness of the fillets. Be sure not to over-bake.

Stuffed Baked Calamari

I remember sitting at a harbour-side restaurant on Mykonos, drinking red wine (so rough you could buff your nails with it) and watching old women in long black skirts slapping squid on the rocks like wet laundry. They then strung the laundry up on a line, like a flap of shirts. As I tucked into my Moussaka I became very aware of those dangling tentacles and felt relieved that, back home, I could buy calamari all neatly packaged in tubes or rings. Even though I can never match the dishes they make with their squid, at least I don't have to beat mine and hang it out with the socks. And yet it still turns out tender and delicious – especially when plumped with a stuffing of *rice* and *spinach*, covered with a chunky *tomato sauce*, baked until butter-soft and then finished off with a blanket of *feta cheese*. This is a super dish for entertaining. You can stuff the calamari in advance and refrigerate it, and the sauce can be whizzed up and set aside until needed. Furthermore, you can dispense with toothpicks and the needlework they involve. I really dislike stitching things closed with toothpicks. Calamari is particularly rubbery when raw, and if the toothpick should inadvertently break off while I'm inserting it, and then inadvertently end up in a guest's stomach, I know that I shall feel terribly advertent and responsible. I have tried the calamari both ways – picked and unpicked – and I find that because the stuffing is not abundant it doesn't leak out. Nor do the tubes explode.

6 cleaned calamari hoods
(or fat tubes) (about 650 g/1½ lb)

STUFFING
30 ml (2 tbsp) olive oil
4–6 spring onions, chopped
1 small red pepper, seeded and diced
125 ml (100 g/3½ oz) long-grain
white rice
300 ml (11 fl oz) hot, salted
chicken stock
5 ml (1 tsp) dried dill
30 ml (2 tbsp) currants
250 ml (30 g/1 oz) finely
shredded spinach

BLENDER TOMATO SAUCE
1 x 410 g (14 oz) can tomatoes
60 ml (4 tbsp) white wine
15 ml (1 tbsp) tomato paste
(see p. 208)
5 ml (1 tsp) sugar
a pinch of salt
1 slim carrot, chopped
1 slim stick table celery,
plus leaves, chopped
1 medium onion, chopped
2–3 cloves garlic, chopped
15 ml (1 tbsp) flour
15 ml (1 tbsp) olive oil

250 g (9 oz) feta cheese, crumbled,
for the topping

Heat the oil in a small saucepan, add the onions and red pepper and, when softening, stir in the rice. Slowly add the stock and remaining ingredients, except the spinach, then cover and simmer for about 20 minutes until the rice is cooked and the liquid has been absorbed. Remove from the stove and immediately add the spinach, tossing until wilted. Spoon the stuffing into the calamari hoods, dividing equally – push it to the bottom and then flatten it out gently. Arrange close together in a baking dish with a lightly oiled base – if working ahead, the calamari can be refrigerated for a couple of hours at this stage, but return to room temperature before baking. To make the sauce, place all the ingredients in a blender and pulse briefly to chop. To bake, pour the sauce over the calamari – it should cover it completely – then cover the dish securely and bake at 160 °C (325 °F, Gas Mark 3) for 1 hour 15 minutes. Sprinkle the feta over the calamari, which will have puffed up into plump little balloons, and then bake, uncovered, for a further 20–25 minutes.

SERVES 4–6.

Spicy Almond Hake in Coriander-cream Sauce

If this title suggests a fancy recipe, it's deceptive. I have simply used it to describe the ingredients in this dish – one of the easiest and tastiest ways of serving baked fish. The sauce, a sensitive mix of *spices* and *herbs*, can be made in advance, while inexpensive *hake* is quite the nicest fish to use as it soaks up the flavours so willingly. Serve with a *tomato-avocado salsa* and fragrant *Indian rice*.

30 ml (2 tbsp) oil

a nut of butter

1 medium onion, finely chopped

1–2 cloves garlic, crushed

5 ml (1 tsp) each ground cumin
and coriander

5 ml (1 tsp) curry powder

2 ml (½ tsp) turmeric

45 ml (3 tbsp) flour

250 ml (9 fl oz) hot fish or
chicken stock

125 ml (4½ fl oz) milk

60 ml (4 tbsp) thick cream

45 ml (3 tbsp) chopped parsley

45 ml (3 tbsp) chopped fresh
coriander leaves

a little salt and lemon juice
to taste

650 g (1½ lb) filleted, skinned
fresh hake (see p. 208)

seasoned flour

flaked almonds*

Heat the oil and butter, add the onion and garlic and, when softened, add the spices and sizzle for a minute. Mix in the flour and, when absorbed, slowly add the stock and milk. Stir over low heat until bubbling and thickened, then remove from heat and add the cream, parsley, coriander, salt and lemon juice. If working ahead, set aside at this stage. Slice the fish into four serving portions or leave in two large fillets. Dust both sides with seasoned flour and place in a baking dish (base lightly oiled) to fit closely without overlapping. Pour the sauce over the fish – it should cover it completely – sprinkle generously with almonds, and bake uncovered at 180 °C (350 °F, Gas Mark 4) for about 25 minutes until the sauce is bubbling merrily, the almonds are lightly browned and the fish is cooked through. SERVES 4.

* Macadamia nuts, lightly toasted and chopped, make a super alternative.

Kingklip with Mushroom and Dill Cream

You can hardly go wrong with this **flop-proof** old favourite – a perfect blend of flavours achieved in one pan. It goes well with **lemony rice** (add finely grated **lemon rind** when cooking the rice) and vegetables or salads.

30 ml (2 tbsp) oil

15 ml (1 tbsp) butter

4 portions kingklip fillets (about 600 g/1¼ lb), or other firm fish

salt and pepper to season

1 leek, thinly sliced

250 g (9 oz) white mushrooms, wiped and sliced

45 ml (3 tbsp) sherry (medium or sweet)

125 ml (4½ fl oz) fish or chicken stock

30 ml (2 tbsp) chopped fresh dill

125 ml (4½ fl oz) cultured sour cream

10 ml (2 tsp) soy sauce

extra dill to garnish

Heat the oil and butter in a heavy-based, wide frying-pan. Add the fish and fry over low heat until just cooked, turning once. Transfer to a baking dish, season lightly and keep warm – if using the oven, have the heat no higher than 160 °C (325 °F, Gas Mark 3). Add the leek, mushrooms, sherry and stock to the pan and simmer uncovered, stirring occasionally, until the mushrooms have softened and the liquid is reduced and syrupy. Add the dill, cream and soy sauce and stir until very hot. Pour the sauce over the fish, garnish with sprigs of dill, and serve immediately.

SERVES 4.

Baked Fish Parcels

These do take time to prepare, as each fish fillet, together with extra goodies for flavour, has to be individually wrapped and securely sealed. However, it is a fun way to serve fish, it's a healthy method, and all the wrapping can be done beforehand and the parcels refrigerated until you want to bake them. Different **herbs**, **spices** and **vegetables** can be used, but the following is a good combination with plenty of flavour and minimal fat.

skinned fish fillets, about
   160 g (5½ oz) each*
salt and lemon juice to taste
garlic, crushed
spring onions, chopped
white mushrooms, wiped and
   thinly sliced
soy sauce
oil
lemon rind, finely grated
toasted sesame seeds

Place the fillet (patted dry) in the centre of a large square (about 40 x 40 cm/16 x 16 in) of lightly oiled greaseproof paper (do not use waxed paper). Sprinkle with a pinch of salt and a few drops of lemon juice. Crush over half a clove of garlic, and top with two spring onions, two or three mushrooms, 5 ml (1 tsp) each soy sauce and oil, then 2 ml (½ tsp) each lemon rind and sesame seeds. Fold the paper from the sides to the middle, roll a few times to secure, then fold the ends, rolling them inwards. Repeat this with each fillet. Place the parcels on a baking tray and if working ahead, refrigerate. Bake at 220 °C (425 °F, Gas Mark 7) for about 25 minutes – the exact time depends on the thickness of the fillets and whether the parcels have been refrigerated or not. To serve, place each puffy, piping hot parcel on a heated dinner plate and serve either plain with just a salad, or with a jug of lemon-butter sauce, new potatoes and vegetables.

* This is pure, lean cuisine and a firm-fleshed fish could be too dry. Hake is ideal for this method of cooking as it has just the right texture and delicacy of flavour.

Low-kilojoule Lemon and Ginger Fish

First poached in a **fragrant stock** and then delicately sauced, the purity of flavours in this dish is exceptional – no cream, no crumbs, no frying. Long, thin fillets of **small kabeljou** are just perfect here.

500 ml (18 fl oz) fish stock
  (or chicken, but it's definitely
  second best)
30 ml (2 tbsp) lemon juice
15 ml (1 tbsp) honey
15 ml (1 tbsp) Thai fish sauce
15 ml (1 tbsp) soy sauce
15 ml (1 tbsp) peeled, finely
  chopped root ginger
2 slim leeks, finely shredded
2 ml (½ tsp) very finely grated
  lemon rind
a good pinch of Chinese Five-Spice
4 skinned fish fillets
  (about 600 g/1¼ lb)
seasoned flour
30 ml (2 tbsp) soft butter
30 ml (2 tbsp) flour
30 ml (2 tbsp) chopped fresh
  coriander leaves
toasted sesame seeds for topping

Use a very wide pan for this dish which will take the fillets in a single layer, and in it bring the stock, lemon juice, honey, fish sauce, soy sauce, ginger, leeks, lemon rind and the Five-Spice to the boil, stirring, then reduce the heat and simmer for 10 minutes. Dust the fish with seasoned flour, shake off the excess, and slide the fillets into the pan. Cover and simmer very gently for about 8 minutes, turning once, until cooked – the exact time depends on the thickness of the fillets. Using a slotted spoon, transfer the fish to a heated serving dish and keep warm. Mash the butter, flour and coriander together to make a paste and drop little pats into the liquid in the pan. You might not need all of it – use just enough to thicken the sauce to a coating consistency. Pour over the fish, sprinkle with sesame seeds and serve with Chinese noodles or rice, and stir-fried vegetables.
SERVES 4.

Fuss-free Fish with a Blender Herb Sauce

Whether you're serving classy kingklip or homely hake, a quick blender sauce will prove a lifesaver when fish is on the menu and you're short on time. This one is really **easy**, jolly **good**, and can be whizzed up in advance.

GREEN HERB SAUCE
250 ml (15 g/½ oz) parsley tufts
10 fresh basil leaves
4 small sprigs fresh marjoram,
    leaves only
2 spring onions, plus some
    green tops, chopped
250 ml (9 fl oz) milk
a little salt
30 ml (2 tbsp) butter
30 ml (2 tbsp) flour
4 fish fillets (about 600 g/1¼ lb),
    poached or steamed
grated Parmesan cheese and
    a few slivers of butter

Place the herbs, onions, milk and salt in blender goblet and blend until finely chopped. Melt the butter in a saucepan, add the flour and stir briefly to cook, then add the herb-milk mixture and stir until bubbling and thick – keep the heat low so as to release the flavours. If necessary, the sauce can be set aside at this stage. Arrange the fish closely in a baking dish (if you've poached it be sure to drain off any liquid first), blanket with sauce, top with cheese and butter and grill until lightly browned.

SERVES 4.

Fish and Asparagus au Gratin

Frozen hake is one of my culinary safety nets. I usually have a box or two in my freezer, and they have rescued me on many an occasion when the thought of cooking dinner made me feeble. Purists might frown on frozen fish, but to my mind the flash-frozen, deep-sea product is far superior to any 'fresh' fish past its prime – dull of eye and fishy of smell. This is a favourite way of treating compact little *hake steaks*, with a topping of *Gruyère cheese* adding a touch of class to otherwise basic ingredients.

1 x 460 g (1 lb) can choice
  asparagus tips and cuts,
  drained, liquid reserved
milk (low-fat if preferred)
30 ml (2 tbsp) each oil and butter
60 ml (4 tbsp) flour
100 g (3½ oz) Cheddar cheese,
  grated
salt and white pepper
20 ml (4 tsp) Dijon mustard
a few spring onions, chopped
1 kg (2¼ lb) frozen, deboned,
  skinless prime hake steaks
  (not fillets)
seasoned flour
grated Gruyère cheese and
  paprika for topping

Add enough milk to the asparagus liquid to make 600 ml (1 pint). Melt the oil and butter, stir in the flour and when smooth slowly add the liquid. Stir over low heat until cooked and medium-thick. Remove from heat and stir in the Cheddar cheese, seasoning and mustard. Set aside at this stage if working ahead. Dust the frozen fish with seasoned flour, rubbing it in lightly and shaking off the excess. Arrange in a single layer in a large dish, with the base and sides lightly oiled. Add the asparagus cuts and scatter with onions. Pour the sauce over to cover, sprinkle with Gruyère and paprika and bake at 180 °C (350 °F, Gas Mark 4) for about 40 minutes – the fish should be cooked through, the cheese melted and the sauce bubbling.

SERVES 6.

* I usually serve this with rice, which can be baked in the oven at the same time. Use the same quantities of rice and water as for stovetop cooking, place in a baking dish lightly brushed with oil, and cover securely. Brown rice will take about 1 hour, white long-grain rice less. Lemony rice always complements fish – add a little grated rind before baking.

Calamari Ratatouille

One doesn't expect to meet **calamari** in a rustic French stew does one, but it's a really happy encounter. **Pasta** is the best partner for this saucy dish, but **rice** is also nice, or you could surround it with fluffy **couscous** for a fine example of fusion cuisine.

30 ml (2 tbsp) each olive oil
  and butter
2 large onions, chopped
3 cloves garlic, crushed
800 g (1¾ lb) cleaned calamari
  tubes, sliced into thin rings
2 x 410 g (14 oz) cans tomatoes,
  chopped, plus juice
125 ml (4½ fl oz) red wine
3 bay leaves
20 ml (4 tsp) tomato paste
  (see p. 208)
400 g (14 oz) brinjals, cubed
  and dégorged
450 g (1 lb) baby marrows, pared
  and sliced (prepared weight)
5 ml (1 tsp) each salt and sugar
2 ml (½ tsp) each dried origanum
  and basil
a handful of chopped parsley
fresh basil and chopped parsley
  to garnish

Heat the oil and butter in a wide-based, heavy saucepan. Add the onions and garlic and soften without browning, then add the calamari and toss until the rings stiffen and turn white. Add the tomatoes, wine, bay leaves and tomato paste, bring to the boil, stirring, then cover and simmer very gently for 30 minutes, by which time the sauce should be thickening but still very plentiful. Stir in the remaining ingredients, then cover and simmer, stirring occasionally, for a further 30–40 minutes or until the vegetables are soft and the calamari is very tender, adding, if necessary, a dash more wine or water to keep the mixture succulent. Alternatively, if the sauce has thinned out, simmer uncovered to reduce. When stirring, be careful not to mash the vegetables – they should remain chunky and identifiable. Remove the bay leaves and check seasoning before serving.
SERVES 6.

Karin's Fish Curry

 This is based on a recipe from a friend who is an inspired cook, always willing to share her most treasured recipes and *never* leaves out the vital, secret ingredient. In order to make the recipe possible for those without access to speciality ingredients, such as *tamarind*, I have made a few alterations, but Karin's curry still turns out absolutely tops. Serve with *Basmati rice* to tie up all the *spicy* fragrances.

30 ml (2 tbsp) oil

15 ml (1 tbsp) butter

2 large onions, finely chopped

25 ml (5 tsp) mild curry powder

5 ml (1 tsp) masala for fish curry

5 ml (1 tsp) each ground cumin
   and turmeric

500 g (1 lb 2 oz) tomatoes, skinned
   and chopped (don't use canned)

10–12 cloves garlic, crushed
   (yes, no fewer)

15 ml (1 tbsp) peeled, chopped
   root ginger

10 ml (2 tsp) tomato paste
   (see p. 208)

375 ml (13 fl oz) fish stock

60 ml (4 tbsp) white wine

7 ml (1½ tsp) salt

10 ml (2 tsp) sugar

about 750 g (1¾ lb) skinned,
   fish fillets, cut into 6 cm (2¼ in)
   squares – use firm fish such
   as Cape salmon, kingklip or
   kabeljou

300 g (11 oz) frozen cooked
   shrimps (rinsed in a colander
   under cold running water)

a few dried curry leaves soaked
   in boiling water until soft
   (about 15 minutes)

plenty of fresh coriander leaves

Heat the oil and butter in a deep, wide-based saucepan and fry the onions until golden. Add the spices and cook gently, stirring, for a few minutes. Add the tomatoes, garlic, ginger, tomato paste, stock, wine and seasoning. Cover and simmer over very low heat for 30 minutes, stirring occasionally. Add the fish and cook gently, uncovered, for 10 minutes, then add the shrimps and cook for 5 minutes. Top with curry leaves and coriander and simmer for a further 5 minutes. By this time the fish should be cooked and the vivid sauce perfectly textured to ladle over the rice, with bowls of chutney, thick yoghurt and a green salad on the side.

SERVES 6.

* Acid ingredients, such as tomatoes, should never be cooked in aluminium saucepans. Use stainless steel, especially when working ahead.

Fish Baked in a Lemon-mushroom Sauce

The finely flavoured **mushroom sauce** can be made in advance and spooned over the uncooked fish just before baking. Serve with parsleyed **rice** and bright **vegetables**.

20 ml (4 tsp) each oil and butter

1 medium onion, finely chopped

200 g (7 oz) white mushrooms, wiped and thinly sliced

5 ml (1 tsp) very finely grated lemon rind

2 ml (½ tsp) dried tarragon, crushed

45 ml (3 tbsp) flour

250 ml (9 fl oz) hot chicken stock

125 ml (4½ fl oz) milk

30 ml (2 tbsp) cream

salt and white pepper

4 skinned fish fillets (about 600 g/1¼ lb) – hake is fine to use here

seasoned flour

Heat the oil and butter, then add the onion and soften without browning. Add the mushrooms, lemon rind and tarragon and toss until mushrooms start to shrink, then sprinkle in the flour. Slowly stir in the stock and milk, then simmer uncovered for a few minutes to thicken the sauce and blend the flavours. Remove from the heat and stir in the cream and seasoning. Dust the fillets with seasoned flour and arrange in a lightly oiled baking dish to fit. Pour the sauce over the top – it should cover the fish generously – and bake uncovered at 180 ˚C (350 ˚F, Gas Mark 4) for about 25 minutes until the sauce is bubbling and the fish is cooked through.

SERVES 4.

# chicken

One day, when I was very small, I was bitten by a cackle of **fowls**. It happened like this. I was spending a holiday with my grandparents on their farm in the Karoo, and every afternoon Granny and I would take a bucket of **grain** – mealie pits and the other things that go into chicken feed – and go to the fowl run, scatter it all over, and then explore the warm nests and collect the eggs. This was a real highlight of my day and on one occasion I decided not to wait for Granny, but to sneak into the run and fill a basket of **eggs** on my own, as a surprise. It was a well-secured enclosure, but, standing on tip-toe, I managed to lift the latch on the gate and crept in. As I headed for the best nest – a soft hollow in the red soil under a thorn tree – the fowls descended on me like a feathered tornado. The silly birds thought my finger-nails were **mealies**.

Hearing my screams, Granny came running to the rescue, and because grown-ups always become angry after they have had a fright, she told me I would have to do without supper because I had been so naughty. Fortunately my beloved old Bushman nanny took pity on me and secretly treated me to high tea. This was a favourite thing between us – she would light a little fire outside and together we would crouch over it and roast unspeakable things – they were probably sheep's intestines. Or something close. Anyway, I always enjoyed whatever it was, and on this occasion the **crisp**, fatty thing/things filled me up, so I didn't go to bed hungry. Funny though – the following day, the fowls went to bed hungry. Right in the middle of the day we had an eclipse of the sun. The homestead, the stables, the whole world was suddenly shrouded in shadow and I was told not to look at the sky. The **fowls** thought night was approaching and they all went to **roost** on their perches on empty stomachs. When the eclipse was over and the sun came out again, they thought it was the following morning. Featherheads.

chicken

Chicken Teriyaki

There are certain comestibles which have such pretty names that they should belong to villages. Like piccalilli. Wouldn't it be jolly to say you enjoyed the piccalillies in Piccalilli? Or the frikkadels in Frikkadel? The meringues in Meringue and the macaroons in Macaroon? **Teriyaki** is such a name. Sadly however, I can't find it in my atlas and I don't think it exists – but it's as good a title as any for a dish which celebrates the happy friendship between **soy sauce, sesame** and **ginger**. Serve these succulent thighs with Chinese **noodles** and stir-fried **vegetables** to add to the fusion of Oriental flavours.

1.2 kg (2¾ lb) chicken thighs,
   trimmed of excess fat
60 ml (4 tbsp) soy sauce
60 ml (4 tbsp) sherry
10 ml (2 tsp) honey
2 cloves garlic, crushed
7 ml (1½ tsp) ground cumin
10 ml (2 tsp) dark sesame oil
10 ml (2 tsp) peeled, chopped
   root ginger
30 ml (2 tbsp) sunflower oil
60 ml (4 tbsp) lemon juice
125 ml (4½ fl oz) chicken stock
sesame seeds
15 ml (1 tbsp) cornflour

Arrange the chicken pieces fairly snugly in a deep dish suitable for both marinating and baking. Mix the soy sauce, sherry, honey, garlic, cumin, sesame oil, ginger, sunflower oil and lemon juice and pour over the chicken. Marinate about 1 hour, turning several times. Just before baking, add the chicken stock. Turn the thighs skin side down, cover and bake at 160 °C (325 °F, Gas Mark 3) for 45 minutes. Turn skin side up, sprinkle with sesame seeds and bake uncovered for a further 45–50 minutes until tender and nicely browned. Use a slotted spoon to transfer the chicken to a warmed serving dish. Pour the juices into a saucepan, stir in cornflour slaked with a dash of water, stir until boiling, then pour over the chicken.
SERVES 5–6.

* This recipe does not require any salt – the soy sauce and stock should season the chicken sufficiently.

Easy Stove-top Indian-style Chicken

'The **four seasons**,' the schoolboy said, 'are Salt, Pepper, Chutney and Chilli.'

30 ml (2 tbsp) oil

1 medium onion, finely chopped

2–3 cloves garlic, crushed

15 ml (1 tbsp) peeled, chopped
root ginger

7 ml (1½ tsp) ground cumin

2 ml (½ tsp) each ground fennel
and turmeric

2 ml (½ tsp) chilli powder
(or more to taste)

500 g (1 lb 2 oz) large, ripe
tomatoes, skinned and coarsely
pulped in a blender

250 ml (9 fl oz) hot chicken stock

a little salt and sugar to taste

200 ml (7 fl oz) coconut milk slaked
with 5 ml (1 tsp) cornflour*

400 g (14 oz) skinless chicken
breast fillets

45–60 ml (3–4 tbsp) fresh coriander
leaves

45–60 ml (3–4 tbsp) dried curry
leaves, soaked for 15 minutes
in boiling water, then drained

Heat the oil in a large frying pan and sauté the onion, garlic and ginger. Stir in the spices and toss briefly until aromatic. Add the tomatoes, 125 ml (4½ fl oz) of the stock, salt, sugar and coconut milk. The sauce will probably curdle slightly but ignore this, just stir for a few minutes, then cover and simmer very gently for 15 minutes, checking and stirring once or twice to make sure that it is only popping and not bubbling away. Open out and flatten the chicken breasts slightly, slice into thin strips across the grain (easily done with a pair of kitchen scissors), add to the pan, stir in the coriander and remaining stock, then cover and simmer for a further 10 minutes or until the chicken is just cooked through. Meanwhile, fry the drained curry leaves in a little oil until crisp. Check seasoning in the curry, spoon into a heated serving dish, and top with the leaves. To tie up all the flavours of India, serve with one of their fragrant rices, chutney and yoghurt.

SERVES 4.

* Home-made coconut milk is far more economical than using a can, and you could, at a pinch, use low-fat milk to lessen the fat-count a little, while still smoothing out the flavour of a curry. Use 250 ml (9 fl oz) milk scalded with 125 ml (40 g/1½ oz) desiccated coconut. Cool, then press through a mesh sieve – this should give you 200 ml (7 fl oz).

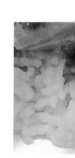

Crunchy Chicken Stir-fry

Spicy chicken with water **chestnuts** and **sprouts** and a topping of **nuts** makes a special meal in minutes. The recipe appears to be lengthy, but don't worry, it just reads that way. Serve on a bed of Chinese **noodles** or **rice**.

400 g (14 oz) skinless chicken
  breast fillets
2 ml (½ tsp) Chinese Five-Spice
2 ml (½ tsp) ground coriander
5 ml (1 tsp) ground ginger
30 ml (2 tbsp) oil
2 sticks table celery, thinly sliced
1 bunch slim spring onions, sliced
1 x 230 g (8 oz) can water
  chestnuts, drained and sliced
2 cloves garlic, crushed
250 ml (60 g/2 oz) bean sprouts

SAUCE
45 ml (3 tbsp) soy sauce
10 ml (2 tsp) honey
30 ml (2 tbsp) sherry
125 ml (4½ fl oz) fresh orange juice
250 ml (9 fl oz) chicken stock
15 ml (1 tbsp) cornflour

toasted almond flakes to garnish

Slice the chicken into thin, diagonal strips across the grain, rub in the spices and set aside for 15 minutes. Heat the oil in a wok or frying pan, add the chicken and stir-fry until just cooked, then push to one side of the pan. Add the celery, onions, chestnuts and garlic to the wok or pan and toss for a few minutes, then bring back the chicken, and add the sauce (all the ingredients should be well stirred together). Simmer until thickened, then stir in the sprouts and, when piping hot, tip into a heated dish and top with plenty of almonds.

SERVES 4–5.

Chicken, Brown Mushroom and Tomato Curry

15 ml (1 tbsp) each oil and butter

1 kg (2¼ lb) chicken thighs
   (8 large), trimmed

salt and pepper to season

1 large onion, finely chopped

4 cloves garlic, crushed

30 ml (2 tbsp) curry powder

10 ml (2 tsp) ground cumin

5 ml (1 tsp) turmeric

15 ml (1 tbsp) peeled, chopped
   root ginger

250 g (9 oz) brown mushrooms,
   wiped and sliced

1 x 410 g (14 oz) can tomatoes,
   chopped, plus juice

2 fat sticks cinnamon

3 bay leaves

a little salt

5 ml (1 tsp) sugar

45 ml (3 tbsp) chutney

125 ml (4½ fl oz) hot chicken stock

60 ml (4 tbsp) fresh coriander
   leaves

Heat the oil and butter in a large frying pan and brown the chicken on both sides – fry skin side first to release the fat. Transfer to a large baking dish and remove the crisped skins – this allows the chicken to absorb the flavours better and avoids a greasy sauce. Turn skinned sides down and season lightly. The thighs should fit fairly closely, but allow space for the chunky sauce – a deep, 28 x 22 cm (11 x 9 in) dish should be just right. Add the onion, garlic, all the ground spices and the ginger to the pan drippings and sauté briefly over low heat – if the drippings are quickly absorbed, add a dash of water. Add the mushrooms, toss until mixed with the spices, then add the remaining ingredients except the coriander. Bring to the boil, stirring, then pour over the chicken – the pieces should be almost completely covered. Check that the cinnamon and bay leaves are well tucked in, cover securely, and bake at 160 ˚C (325 ˚F, Gas Mark 3) for 1 hour 15 minutes. Turn the chicken and bake, uncovered, for a further 15 minutes or until tender and the sauce is nicely reduced. Use a slotted spoon to transfer the chicken to a heated serving dish. Remove the bay leaves and cinnamon sticks from the sauce, stir in the coriander, pour over the chicken and serve with Basmati rice and a bowl of thick, plain yoghurt.

SERVES 4–6.

Saucy Oriental Orange and Ginger Chicken

Capture a waft of the Orient in this super **sauce**, subtly flavoured with **ginger** and **lemon grass**. The latter is a wonderful herb which grows willingly, needs little attention, and adds an intriguing flavour to so many dishes.

8 chicken thighs (about 1 kg/ 2¼ lb), trimmed of excess fat
30 ml (2 tbsp) soy sauce
30 ml (2 tbsp) sherry
30 ml (2 tbsp) honey
30 ml (2 tbsp) lemon juice
15 ml (1 tbsp) oil
4 stalks lemon grass (fleshy white part, bruised, outer layer removed)
250 ml (9 fl oz) fresh orange juice
250 ml (9 fl oz) chicken stock
6–8 spring onions, chopped
15 ml (1 tbsp) peeled, chopped root ginger
2–3 cloves garlic, crushed
5 ml (1 tsp) finely grated orange rind
30 ml (2 tbsp) cornflour
toasted sesame seeds for topping

Place the chicken in a baking dish – the thighs should fit snugly, but the dish should be deep enough to take the sauce. Mix the soy sauce, sherry, honey, lemon juice and oil, pour over the chicken, turning several times to coat well, then let it stand for about 45 minutes. Turn skin side down, tuck in lemon grass and bake, covered, at 160 °C (325 °F, Gas Mark 3) for 45 minutes. Meanwhile, stir together the remaining ingredients to make the sauce. Turn the chicken skin side up, pour the sauce over, then turn the oven up to 200 °C (400 °F, Gas Mark 6). (The reason for this is that the sauce is cold, and it will take too long to come to a bubble at the initial lower temperature.) Bake uncovered for about 45 minutes, basting once or twice, until the chicken is tender and browned and the sauce has thickened. Switch off the oven and leave for 10 minutes to settle, then spoon the chicken into a heated serving dish, discard the lemon grass, pour sauce over and sprinkle generously with sesame seeds.
SERVES 4–6.

Chicken Tajine with Prunes and Spicy Couscous

I've never been to Morocco, but I have stood on the Rock of Gibraltar with some Barbary apes. Together we looked across to the hazy blue Rif Mountains in North Africa, and had a good sniff. Call me fanciful, but was that a hint of *spice* on the breeze? It certainly wasn't an ape. I reckon it was *saffron* and *ginger*, *cinnamon* and *cumin*, all whiffed together with *mint* and *licorice* and *sage*. Morocco, after all, is not far from Gibraltar – just across the blue Mediterranean with its flotilla of boats and ferries and possibly a flying carpet or two – and being lunch-time, hundreds of families must have been settling onto poufs at low round tables and dipping into hot, sweet-sour tajines. So who's to say the perfumes were not wafting over? It's such a pity that I never got to boarding a carpet in order to experience the country personally, because few cooks outside Morocco can copy their vibrant cuisine. Not only are their utensils unique (like the round tajine with its pointed lid), but they have a way of mixing unlikely ingredients – things like meat with dates and nuts and pickled lemons and quinces – to create taste sensations unlike any other. The following simplified recipe incorporates some of their favoured ingredients to offer a glimpse of what their country has to offer.

150 g (5½ oz) pitted prunes
15 ml (1 tbsp) each oil and butter
8 large chicken thighs, skinned
  (1 kg/2¼ lb skinned weight)
1 medium onion, finely chopped
4 cloves garlic, crushed
15 ml (1 tbsp) peeled, chopped
  root ginger
7 ml (1½ tsp) cumin seeds
5 ml (1 tsp) ground cinnamon
1 ml (¼ tsp) grated nutmeg
500 g (1 lb 2 oz) ripe tomatoes
a large pinch of saffron infused in
  30 ml (2 tbsp) hot water
250 ml (9 fl oz) chicken stock
15 ml (1 tbsp) tomato paste
  (see p. 208)
3 x 5 cm (2 in) strips lemon peel
30 ml (2 tbsp) honey
2 fat sticks cinnamon
flaked almonds

SPICY COUSCOUS
30 ml (2 tbsp) oil
a few spring onions, chopped
2 ml (½ tsp) each ground cumin,
  fennel and cinnamon
550 ml (19 fl oz) hot chicken stock
90 ml (6 tbsp) currants
5 ml (1 tsp) finely grated lemon rind
a pinch each of salt and sugar
375 ml (255 g/9 oz) quick-cooking
  couscous
a small nut of butter
chopped fresh coriander leaves

Pour boiling water over the prunes (I add a teabag for added flavour, but this is optional) and leave to soak – do not stir, as pitted prunes are quite soft and you don't want to mash them. Heat the oil and butter and seal the chicken on both sides. Arrange the pieces skinned sides down in a large baking dish to fit comfortably, and deep enough to allow for the sauce. Season. Add the onion, garlic and spices to the pan drippings and toss briefly until sizzling and smelling fabulous (add a dash of water if necessary). Skin and chop the tomatoes, and add, together with the saffron, stock, tomato paste and lemon peel. Bring to the boil, stirring to break up the tomatoes, then pour the sauce over the chicken. Tuck in the cinnamon sticks, cover securely, and bake at 160 ˚C (325 ˚F, Gas Mark 3) for 1 hour 15 minutes. Remove the cinnamon and lemon peel, turn the chicken, stir in the drained prunes and honey, scatter liberally with almonds and bake, uncovered, for a further 15–20 minutes.

Heat the oil in a wide-based saucepan, add the onions and spices and toss for a minute or two to release the flavours. Add the stock, currants, lemon rind and seasoning and bring to the boil. Add the couscous, stir to mix, then remove from the heat and stand, covered, for 5 minutes. Fork in the butter and coriander.

Place the chicken on a large, heated platter, pour the sauce over and surround with the couscous.
SERVES 6–8.

Mexican Chicken with Corn and Olives

 Think **Mexican food** and think *corn* and *chillies*, *tomatoes* and *avocados*, *spices* and *herbs*, bacon and olives, peanuts, raisins and chocolate – the last three astonishingly combined with turkey. It certainly is a most colourful cuisine, and although there are no alarming ingredients in the following dish, it turns out as bright as a rainbow. Serve with *rice* and *avocado-chilli salsa*.

a few rashers of rindless,
   lean bacon, chopped
8 large well-trimmed chicken
   thighs (1 kg/2¼ lb)
2 medium onions, chopped
2–3 cloves garlic, crushed
1 large green pepper, seeded
   and diced
5 ml (1 tsp) chilli powder
   (or to taste)
15 ml (1 tbsp) flour
1 x 410 g (14 oz) can tomatoes,
   chopped, plus juice
60 ml (4 tbsp) red wine
125 ml (4½ fl oz) chicken stock
a little salt and a pinch of sugar
a handful of chopped parsley
5 ml (1 tsp) dried origanum
1 x 270 g (10 oz) can corn kernels,
   drained
slivered black olives to garnish

Fry the bacon in a large pan smeared with oil, then transfer it to a large baking dish (about 28 x 22 cm/11 x 9 in). Place the chicken in the pan and brown on both sides – do this in two batches – then transfer it to the dish with the bacon, and season lightly. Soften the onions, garlic and green pepper in the pan drippings (if necessary, add a dash of water), sprinkle in the chilli powder and stir in the flour. When absorbed, add the remaining ingredients, except the corn and olives, bring to the boil, stirring, then pour the sauce over the chicken. Cover and bake at 160 °C (325 °F, Gas Mark 3) for 1 hour. Stir in the corn, and bake uncovered for a further 15 minutes until the chicken is tender and the sauce has thickened. If necessary, blot the surface with a paper towel to remove any fat. Top with olives.

AVOCADO-CHILLI SALSA:

Dice one large avocado and sprinkle the flesh with lemon juice. Fold in one small red chilli, seeded and chopped; two spring onions, chopped; one medium tomato, chopped; a few coriander leaves and seasoning to taste.

SERVES 4–6.

Cheese-topped Chicken and Vegetable Bake

Simply a different way with breasts; no mushrooms, no cream, no curry, no last-minute frying. These breasts are conveniently oven-baked, which can be a dodgy method because they're a delicate cut and can easily become stringy and tough. Prepared this way, however, the generous *tomato-marrow* sauce takes care of their succulence, while the topping of melted *Mozzarella* keeps the whole lot snugly covered. This chicken dish goes really well with *pasta* and a *spinach and bacon salad*.

800 g (1¾ lb) skinless chicken
  breast fillets
15 ml (1 tbsp) each olive oil
  and butter
salt and pepper
5 ml (1 tsp) mixed dried
  Italian herbs
2 medium leeks, thinly sliced
3–4 cloves garlic, crushed
1 x 410 g (14 oz) can tomatoes,
  chopped, plus juice
15 ml (1 tbsp) tomato paste
  (see p. 208)
200 g (7 oz) baby marrows,
  pared, halved and diced
  (prepared weight)
2 sticks table celery, plus
  leaves, chopped
a little salt
5 ml (1 tsp) sugar
250 ml (9 fl oz) chicken stock
200–300 g (7–11 oz) Mozzarella
  cheese, thinly sliced

Make a few diagonal slashes on the skinned side of the breasts, then seal quickly on both sides in hot oil and butter – use a large pan. Transfer the chicken to a baking dish to fit fairly closely – the size of the dish depends on the number of breasts – 800 g (1¾ lb) could mean 8 large or 12 small. Sprinkle with seasoning and herbs. If necessary, add an extra dash of oil to the pan, then sauté the leeks and garlic. Add the remaining ingredients, except the cheese, and simmer, covered, for about 25 minutes, stirring occasionally, until the vegetables are soft and the sauce has thickened. Pour the sauce over the breasts – they should be completely covered. Bake uncovered at 180 °C (350 °F, Gas Mark 4) for 20 minutes – the sauce should have started to bubble round the edges. Quickly cover with the cheese – you could add a sprinkling of paprika for colour, although this isn't strictly Italian – and bake for a further 20 minutes or until the cheese has spread and melted and the chicken is cooked through.

SERVES 6–8.

Spicy, Fruity Chutney Chicken

This dish is dead easy, yet delicious. Serve with **yellow rice** and **broccoli** for a lovely colour splash.

1 kg (2¼ lb) chicken pieces
12 pickling-sized onions, peeled
125 ml (4½ fl oz) mild fruit chutney
250 ml (9 fl oz) fresh orange juice
10 ml (2 tsp) curry powder
2 ml (½ tsp) each ground
    cinnamon, ginger and turmeric
5 ml (1 tsp) salt
4 cloves
60 ml (4 tbsp) sultanas
30 ml (2 tbsp) flour
60 ml (4 tbsp) water

Remove any excess fat from the chicken and halve the breasts, if large. Arrange in a single layer in a baking dish, the base brushed with oil. Tuck the onions in-between the chicken pieces. Mix all the remaining ingredients, stirring well until the flour disappears – simply press any little lumps against the side of the mixing jug with a wooden spoon. When smooth, pour over the chicken, cover and bake at 160 °C (325 °F, Gas Mark 3) for 1 hour. Uncover – expect the chicken to look rather pale and uninteresting at this stage, but do not be alarmed. Give it a quick baste with the juices, then bake, uncovered, for about 25 minutes more, until the chicken is browned, the onions are soft, and the sauce is very bubbly and reduced. Discard the cloves if you see them, then serve.

SERVES 4–5.

Chicken Baked in Orange and Rosemary Cream Sauce

This dish is specially devised for easy entertaining.

The creamy sauce splashed with *mustard*, *honey* and

brandy is just so different from the usual sauces which

blanket chicken breasts that guests are sure to quiz you about

the recipe. Don't tell them. It's so simple and quick, they might

think you hadn't taken much trouble over their dinner, which you

hadn't. Serve on a platter surrounded with *fragrant rice* to soak

up the rich sauce, and pass a glossy *spinach and mushroom salad.*

15 ml (1 tbsp) each oil and butter

2 medium leeks, finely shredded

2 cloves garlic, crushed

15 ml (1 tbsp) finely chopped fresh
rosemary leaves

2 ml (½ tsp) finely grated
orange rind

45 ml (3 tbsp) flour
(absolutely level)

125 ml (4½ fl oz) fresh orange juice

250 ml (9 fl oz) hot chicken stock

15 ml (1 tbsp) Dijon mustard

15 ml (1 tbsp) brandy

15 ml (1 tbsp) honey

125 ml (4½ fl oz) thick cream

a little salt

4 large skinless chicken breast
fillets (400–500 g/14 oz–1 lb 2 oz)

toasted almond flakes or snipped
chives to garnish

To make the sauce, heat the oil and butter, add the leeks and garlic and soften without browning. Add the rosemary, orange rind and flour and, when the latter is absorbed, slowly stir in the juice and stock. Bring to the boil, stirring, then reduce heat and add the mustard, brandy, honey, cream and salt. Allow to bubble gently for about 5 minutes to concentrate the flavour and to reduce the sauce to the consistency of light cream. Make a few diagonal slashes across the chicken breasts, on the side from which the skin was removed, and arrange fairly close together in a baking dish with a base brushed with oil. Season lightly and pour sauce over to cover completely. Bake uncovered at 160 ˚C (325 ˚F, Gas Mark 3) for 45 minutes until the sauce is bubbling and the chicken is cooked through. (Chicken breasts will toughen if cooked at a high temperature, or for too long.) Sprinkle with almonds or chives.

SERVES 4, and can easily be doubled.

Thai-style Chicken and Mushroom Curry

Fragrant curries are always popular and this is a favourite version. Although it should be served as soon as it is ready, the ingredients can be prepared in advance, and the final cook-up is pretty quick. Thickening the sauce at the end may not be traditional, but it avoids a 'soupy' end result, which can happen when using coconut milk. Serve on a bed of *Oriental noodles* or *fragrant rice*.

30 ml (2 tbsp) oil
10 ml (2 tsp) peeled, chopped
  root ginger
5 ml (1 tsp) ground cumin
2 stalks lemon grass
  (fleshy white part, bruised,
  outer layer removed)
250 g (9 oz) white mushrooms,
  wiped and sliced
15–30 ml (1–2 tbsp) green
  curry paste*
300 ml (11 fl oz) canned
  coconut milk
125 ml (4½ fl oz) chicken stock
10 ml (2 tsp) soy sauce
15 ml (1 tbsp) Thai fish sauce
4–6 spring onions, chopped
400 g (14 oz) skinless chicken
  breast fillets, thinly sliced
  across the grain
20 ml (4 tsp) cornflour
45 ml (3 tbsp) fresh coriander
  leaves
roasted cashew nuts to garnish

Heat the oil in a large frying pan. Add the ginger, cumin, lemon grass and mushrooms and stir-fry over low heat until the mushrooms soften. Stir in the curry paste and cook for 1–2 minutes. Add the coconut milk, 100 ml (3½ fl oz) of the stock, soy sauce, fish sauce and spring onions. Bring to the boil, then add the chicken. Reduce the heat and simmer, uncovered, stirring occasionally, for about 10 minutes or until the chicken is cooked. Slake the cornflour with the remaining stock, add to the pan, add the coriander, and stir until bubbling and slightly thickened. Remove the lemon grass and sprinkle with cashews.

MAKES 4 MODEST SERVINGS.

* 15 ml (1 tbsp) provides a very mild tingle – increase according to taste.

meat

There are certain aromas that, throughout one's life, instantly evoke memories of one's childhood. For each of us these nostalgic **aromas** are unique, conjuring up a personal recollection of a scene, an encounter, or a special occasion, and often the sentiment is associated with food. It could be the sweet, yeasty waft from home-made bread billowing in the oven; the appalling wake-up call of burnt porridge at boarding school; or the thyme-drenched stuffing in the Christmas turkey, filling the house with its promise of presents and crackers. One of the most poignant memories in my book is that of **chops** being grilled for breakfast on a farm in the Karoo.

The sun rises swiftly in this part of the world because there are no clouds to block its path. It simply soars up over the horizon, bouncing with energy and a dazzle of smiles at the prospect of yet another molten day. As a child, this was a magical time for me. A time to ride my horse down the avenue of thorn trees, past the cow-shed where warm milk was already being whooshed into pails, and into the early-morning silence of a vast, dry, scrubby and endless stretch of land with nothing to see but a straggle of sheep, a few plodding tortoises, basking lizards, and occasionally a snake. It was a childhood cameo etched with a sense of freedom and lightness that lives forever in my mind.

On the ride back, I would rein in just short of the farmhouse for a swim in a muddy, green-water dam with bulbous-eyed frogs; pick some furry figs from the tree on the bank; and then head home, ravenous. And this is the magic memory: eating a sun-drenched fig at dawn after a cold swim, as we trotted past a grid-iron laden with smouldering **lamb** chops being grilled for breakfast. As the fat spattered onto the coals, wisps of perfumed smoke spiralled and disappeared into the blue beyond the stables. Minutes later the chops would be placed on the polished diningroom table, along with porridge and thick cream and humpy home-made bread. For lunch it would be **roast** lamb, and for supper perhaps fried liver, or **sausage** and eggs. That was then. These days a roast is a treat, and meat three times a day is unheard of. It's due to a change of lifestyle, appetites, and cost – and therefore most of the recipes in this chapter are designed to stretch servings of meat with vegetables and sauces. A pity perhaps, but the passage of time inevitably requires one to chop, and to change.

meat

Casseroled Lamb Curry

A commendable curry, which conveniently does itself to a turn in the oven. The sauce is **thick and spicy**, interesting but not fiery, and rich but not greasy. Although shoulder or neck slices make the best **stews**, they are bony and bulky and so I have used chump chops – far more manageable, and the tiny marrow bones add the necessary succulence.

8 large chump chops
   (thick slices of leg of lamb)
30 ml (2 tbsp) oil
2 medium onions, chopped
3 cloves garlic, crushed
15 ml (1 tbsp) curry powder
10 ml (2 tsp) peeled,
   chopped root ginger
5 ml (1 tsp) each ground cumin,
   coriander and turmeric
4 cloves
2 sticks cinnamon
30 ml (2 tbsp) flour
250 ml (9 fl oz) hot beef stock
125 ml (4½ fl oz) tomato purée
   (see p. 208)
5 ml (1 tsp) salt
10 ml (2 tsp) sugar
2 large carrots, finely diced
30 ml (2 tbsp) chutney
2 bay leaves

Slice each chop into 3–4 pieces, removing all the rind and fat, but leaving the small marrow bone in the centres of some of the slices. Trimmed weight should be about 900 g (2 lb). Heat the oil in a large frying pan and braise onions, garlic and spices over low heat for a few minutes – if too dry add a dash of water. Increase the heat, add lamb and toss until starting to fry, then sprinkle in the flour and when absorbed slowly stir in remaining ingredients. Bring to the boil, then transfer to a medium-sized baking dish. Cover and bake at 160 °C (325 °F, Gas Mark 3) for 1 hour 15 minutes, then uncover and bake for a further 20 minutes until the lamb is butter-soft and the sauce thickened. Curries are often tastier when made in advance, therefore, if time allows, transfer to a suitable container when cooled, remove spices, and refrigerate overnight. Reheat, covered, at 160 °C (325 °F, Gas Mark 3) until bubbling.
SERVES 4–6.

Citrus and Ginger Pork Chop Bake

Tender **chops** in a tangy sauce. Serve simply, with **mash** and cabbage salad, or smarten up for guests with swirls of **creamed potatoes** and stir-fried **vegetables**. The chops are a pleasure either way.

8 pork rib or loin chops,
    about 1 kg (2¼ lb)
seasoned flour
300 ml (11 fl oz) fresh orange juice
30 ml (2 tbsp) soy sauce
15 ml (1 tbsp) lemon juice
10 ml (2 tsp) peeled,
    chopped root ginger
45 ml (3 tbsp) orange marmalade
1 medium onion, finely chopped
5 ml (1 tsp) mustard powder
2 cloves garlic, crushed
30 ml (2 tbsp) sherry
a large pinch of sugar
60 ml (4 tbsp) sultanas

Remove rind and excess fat from chops, roll in seasoned flour and fry lightly on both sides in a little oil until just golden-brown. Arrange in a large baking dish to fit closely without overlapping. Add the remaining ingredients, except the sultanas, to the frying pan and stir over low heat until combined. Pour over the chops, cover securely, and bake at 160 °C (325 °F, Gas Mark 3) for 1 hour. Add sultanas and bake, covered, for a further 15 minutes, by which time the chops should be beautifully tender and the sauce reduced and thickened.

SERVES 6–8.

Lamb Chops Baked in a Zesty Sauce

A homely, reliable old-timer to satisfy hearty appetites. The acid ingredients in the **sweet-sour sauce** tenderize the meat, resulting in **succulent chops** with a tasty tang to the flavour.

8 chump chops, about 1.2 kg
   (2¾ lb), trimmed of fat
seasoned flour
30–45 ml (2–3 tbsp) oil
2 medium onions, chopped
3 cloves garlic, crushed
10 ml (2 tsp) curry powder
400 ml (14 fl oz) beef stock
10 ml (2 tsp) Worcestershire sauce
60 ml (4 tbsp) tomato sauce
30 ml (2 tbsp) chutney
15 ml (1 tbsp) brown vinegar
15 ml (1 tbsp) soft brown sugar
2 medium carrots, diced
90 ml (6 tbsp) chopped parsley
45 ml (3 tbsp) seedless raisins

Snip edges of chops to prevent curling, dust with seasoned flour, and brown on both sides in the oil. You'll need to do this in batches in a large, heavy frying pan. As they brown, remove chops to a baking dish (glass or earthenware, not a baking tin) with base lightly oiled. They should fit quite snugly. Reduce heat and add onions, garlic and curry powder to pan – if necessary add a dash of water, to allow onions to sweat without scorching. Stir in remaining ingredients, bring to the boil, and then pour over chops. Cover and bake at 160 °C (325 °F, Gas Mark 3) for 1 hour. Turn and bake uncovered for a further 20 minutes or until sauce is reduced, slightly syrupy and a good, rich colour.
SERVES 6–8.

Fillet Steaks with a Chunky Mushroom-Wine Sauce

There's nothing new about **steak** in a **mushroom sauce**, but where this recipe scores is in its speed and simplicity. The ingredients for the sauce are mixed in advance, and then stirred into the pan after frying the steaks. The mushroom and **cucumber** quickly release their fresh flavours into the **wine** and stock, and the result is a prime dish to serve when time is tight.

600 g (1¼ lb) centre-cut fillet of beef
crushed garlic
coarsely ground black peppercorns
30 ml (2 tbsp) oil
10 ml (2 tsp) butter

SAUCE
125 ml (4½ fl oz) red wine
15 ml (1 tbsp) cornflour
4–6 spring onions, chopped
125 g (4½ oz) white mushrooms,
   wiped and finely chopped
125 g (4½ oz) English cucumber,
   pared, seeded and diced
250 ml (9 fl oz) beef stock
15 ml (1 tbsp) soy sauce
30 ml (2 tbsp) cream

First make the sauce: stir the wine with the cornflour until smooth, then mix with the remaining sauce ingredients and refrigerate.

Slice the beef into steaks – 4 medium, or 6 mean little ones. Sprinkle the garlic and pepper onto both sides and press in with the heel of your palm – take care not to flatten them. Heat the oil and butter in a large, heavy frying pan, add steaks and cook until as done as you like them to be, and browned on both sides, turning once only. Remove to a serving platter and keep warm. Reduce the heat, add the sauce to the pan and stir until bubbling, glossy and thickened. Check the seasoning – despite the inclusion of soy sauce and stock, you might need a pinch of salt. Pour the sauce over the steaks and serve immediately.
SERVES 4–6.

Greek-style Lamb with Vegetables and Herbs

This is a full-bodied, buxom **stew** combining **lamb knuckles** and lots of **vegetables**, slow-simmered to perfection in a **herby-tomato-wine** sauce. Serve with **rice** and cinnamon-pumpkin, or buttered **shell noodles**, a **roasted pepper** salad, and a pot of **yoghurt** blended with chives and honey. To allow the full flavour to develop, make in advance and reheat.

800 g–1 kg (1¾–2¼ lb) sliced
   lamb knuckles
30 ml (2 tbsp) oil and a nut of butter
2 medium onions, finely chopped
3 cloves garlic, crushed
400 g (14 oz) brinjals, cubed
   and dégorged
400 g (14 oz) baby marrows,
   pared and sliced
3 medium carrots, diced
10 ml (2 tsp) dried origanum
375 ml (13 fl oz) beef stock
200 ml (7 fl oz) tomato purée
   (see p. 208)
125 ml (4½ fl oz) red wine
15 ml (1 tbsp) honey
4 bay leaves
3 sprigs fresh rosemary
salt and pepper
fresh coriander, basil or parsley
   (if all else fails) to garnish

Heat the oil and butter in a very large saucepan, add lamb and brown well. Remove lamb, reduce heat, add onions to pan and sauté lightly, then add vegetables and origanum and toss for a few minutes over low heat. Return lamb, add remaining ingredients, stir to mix and moisten everything, then cover and simmer very gently for about 1 hour, stirring occasionally, until the lamb is tender and the sauce thick but plentiful. (Be sure not to cook rapidly – the stew should just pop gently all the while.) Remove bay leaves and rosemary stalks before serving – the leaves will have melted into the stew. If necessary, add a dash more stock, check seasoning, and garnish.
SERVES 5–6.

Old-fashioned Beef and Onion Casserole

This is comfort food, pure and simple. All you need do is assemble a couple of basic ingredients, pop the dish into the oven, and forget about it. The result is pure nostalgia – **tender steak** in a **savoury gravy**, to serve with homespun **mash** and **vegetables**.

10 ml (2 tsp) mustard powder

2 ml (½ tsp) salt

5 ml (1 tsp) mixed dried herbs

2 cloves garlic, chopped

6 pieces of lean, shoulder braising steak, about 600 g (1¼ lb)

2 medium onions, sliced into rings

3 bay leaves

4 cloves

30 ml (2 tbsp) flour

5 ml (1 tsp) Worcestershire sauce

15 ml (1 tbsp) tomato paste (see p. 208)

15 ml (1 tbsp) soy sauce

5 ml (1 tsp) sugar

375 ml (13 fl oz) beef stock

30 ml (2 tbsp) chutney

Mix mustard powder, salt, herbs and garlic. Using a flat-bladed knife, press into one side of each piece of steak, then place, herbed side up, in a baking dish (not a roasting tin), base lightly oiled, to fit fairly closely. Cover with onion rings. Add bay leaves and cloves. Whisk together remaining ingredients and pour over – the meat should be almost submerged. Cover very securely and bake at 160 °C (325 °F, Gas Mark 3) for 1½ hours. Uncover and bake until sauce is sufficiently reduced and thickened – the time depends on the size of the baking dish, but bank on about 30 minutes. Comfort dishes require no garnish – simply remove bay leaves and cloves, if you can find them.

4 ADULT, OR 6 BUDGET SERVINGS.

Layered Brinjal and Mince Bake

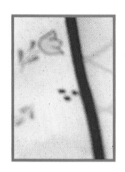

This is not unlike moussaka, but the recipe is so different from the traditional dish that I simply have to give it another name. Any self-respecting moussaka takes lengthy preparation and includes egg yolks, a rich cheese sauce, minced lamb and butter, whereas this variation is considerably lighter and simpler. But it's delicious nevertheless, served with a *green salad* tucked with *olives*, *crusty bread* and a carafe of *red wine*.

1 kg (2¼ lb) small to medium
  brinjals, sliced into 10 mm (⅜ in)
  rounds and dégorged
olive oil
1 large onion, chopped
1 kg (2¼ lb) lean beef mince
250 ml (9 fl oz) tomato purée
  (see p. 208)
125 ml (4½ fl oz) red wine
3 cloves garlic, crushed
5 ml (1 tsp) dried origanum
7 ml (1½ tsp) salt
a large pinch of sugar
2 ml (½ tsp) ground cinnamon
a handful of chopped parsley
2 egg whites

SAUCE
45 ml (3 tbsp) soft butter
75 ml (5 tbsp) flour
750 ml (1¼ pints) milk
  (low-fat may be used)
2 ml (½ tsp) grated nutmeg
2 ml (½ tsp) salt
45 ml (3 tbsp) grated
  Parmesan cheese

extra grated Parmesan cheese for
  topping

Arrange rinsed and dried brinjal slices in a single layer on two baking trays lined with baking paper, brush with oil, place low down in the oven, switch on grill and allow to brown and soften, turning once, and brushing again with oil – this takes about 20 minutes.

Meanwhile, heat 30 ml (2 tbsp) oil in a large frying pan. Fry the onion lightly, then add mince and toss until browned. Add remaining ingredients except the egg whites. Cover and simmer gently, stirring occasionally, for about 25 minutes – the mixture should be fairly dry. To make the short-cut sauce, place all the ingredients in a blender and blend at high speed – the mixture will not be smooth at this stage. Pour into a heavy saucepan rinsed out with cold water, and stir over low heat until just bubbling, smooth and thickened. Cover the base of a 20 x 30 cm (6 x 12 in) baking dish with half the brinjal slices. Whisk egg whites lightly, fold into meat sauce, spoon over the brinjal layer, then cover with remaining brinjals. Pour white sauce over, sprinkle with extra cheese, and bake at 180 °C (350 °F, Gas Mark 4) for 40 minutes. Switch off oven heat and leave for 20 minutes to settle, then serve sliced into large squares.
SERVES 8.

Saucy Lamb Chops

When it comes to serving chops, one has to choose between having them pink and grilled, or well-done and sauced. Most home cooks plump for the latter option, as grilling them perfectly can be tricky; simmering them to melt-in-the-mouth tenderness on top of the stove is much simpler. Both the following recipes require loin chops, which have a short T-shaped bone at the top. Once the rind and excess fat have been removed, the 'tail' end can be wrapped around to form a small, neat shape. Done this way, one large frying pan will accommodate a generous number of chops.

1 LAMB CHOPS WITH MUSHROOMS AND PORT

12 lamb loin chops, about 1 kg (2¼ lb)
salt and dried thyme
60 ml (4 tbsp) oil
2 medium onions, finely chopped
3 cloves garlic, crushed
400 g (14 oz) brown mushrooms, wiped and chopped
30 ml (2 tbsp) flour
60 ml (4 tbsp) soy sauce
60 ml (4 tbsp) port
500 ml (18 fl oz) beef stock
7 ml (1½ tsp) finely grated orange rind

Trim and 'wrap' chops as described above. Brown quickly on both sides in a large frying pan just smeared with oil, then remove to a large plate and sprinkle with a little salt and crushed thyme. Add the oil to the pan together with the onions, garlic and mushrooms and toss until softening. Sprinkle in the flour, and when absorbed stir in the remaining ingredients. When bubbling, return chops, reduce heat, cover and simmer very gently for about 20 minutes until tender, turning once. Using a slotted spoon, transfer the chops to a large, heated serving dish. Simmer sauce, uncovered, for a few minutes until thickened, then pour over the chops and serve.

SERVES 6.

Saucy Lamb Chops

**2   LAMB CHOPS IN SHERRY
AND MUSTARD SAUCE**

12 lamb loin chops, about
   1 kg (2¼ lb)
30 ml (2 tbsp) oil
1 medium onion, finely chopped
30 ml (2 tbsp) flour
5 ml (1 tsp) dried thyme
500 ml (18 fl oz) hot beef stock
30 ml (2 tbsp) tomato paste
   (see p. 208)
60 ml (4 tbsp) sherry
20–30 ml (4–6 tsp) wholegrain
   mustard
10 ml (2 tsp) Worcestershire sauce
a large pinch each of salt
   and sugar

Trim and 'wrap' chops as described on page 123. Heat the oil in a heavy frying pan large enough to take the chops in a single layer, and brown them on both sides – keep the heat low so that they will be almost cooked through. Remove the chops, and brown the onion in the pan drippings. Add the flour and thyme, and when absorbed, stir in the stock and then the remaining ingredients. Bring to the boil, stirring, then reduce heat to very low and return chops to the pan. Cover and simmer gently for about 15 minutes, or until very tender, turning once.

SERVES 6.

Savoury Veal and Vegetables

A bright and chunky **veal bake**, flavoured with **mustard** and **orange**. Unpretentious and uncomplicated, it makes a good choice for an informal meal, served on **rice** or **couscous**.

30 ml (2 tbsp) oil

2–3 rashers lean shoulder bacon, diced

500 g (1 lb 2 oz) braising veal, cut into small cubes, patted dry

1 large onion, chopped

2 medium carrots, finely diced

2 sticks table celery, chopped, plus some leaves

2 ml (½ tsp) turmeric

5 ml (1 tsp) dried tarragon, crushed between your fingers

30 ml (2 tbsp) flour

125 ml (4½ fl oz) fresh orange juice

2 ml (½ tsp) finely grated orange rind

250 ml (9 fl oz) chicken stock

2 ml (½ tsp) salt

10 ml (2 tsp) honey

15 ml (1 tbsp) wholegrain mustard

5 ml (1 tsp) Dijon mustard

15 ml (1 tbsp) brandy

fresh tarragon leaves or chopped parsley to garnish

Heat the oil in a large frying pan, add bacon and fry briefly, then add veal in small batches, tossing all the while until lightly browned. Using a slotted spoon, remove to a medium-sized baking dish – a deep, 23 cm (9 in) pie dish is ideal – no bigger, or the sauce will simmer away. Reduce heat and add onion, carrots and celery to the pan. If it is dry, add a dash of water and/or a nut of butter. Toss for a few minutes until beginning to soften, then sprinkle in turmeric, tarragon and flour. When absorbed, add remaining ingredients, stirring until the sauce thickens and comes to the boil. Pour over veal, stir to mix, then cover securely and bake at 160 °C (325 °F, Gas Mark 3) for 1 hour 15 minutes. Sprinkle with the garnish.

SERVES 4–5.

pasta

Many people feel that pasta is the greatest legacy bestowed by **Italy** on the human race. And that includes Michaelangelo, the Colosseum, and all the Roman roads. Not everyone will agree with this of course, but no one can deny that **pasta** is enormously popular and is eaten all over the world. Somehow, though, one feels that dining on pasta in Italy is the ultimate, and the **spaghetti** I had in Venice remains one of my fondest memories. Actually, it wasn't the spaghetti – which wasn't particularly good – it was the sparrows. Sharing my lunch with a flock of little Italian passero at a sidewalk trattoria beside the Grand Canal became a daily delight.

Like a flutter of feathers shaken from a pillow on high, they would descend on my table, mince across the cloth to my plate, snitch a strand of pasta, and then fly off to build a nest of classical, baroque beauty on top of one of those soaring domes.

At least that's what I like to think. And when their chicks hatched out in their **fettucine**-style nests, they would feed on the drops of **olive oil**, perhaps a tomato pip or two, a sliver of anchovy, a peck of **garlic** – all the healthy things that had stuck to the pasta which their parents had pinched. On such a diet they grew big and strong. Italian sparrows to the back teeth. Which brings me back to olive oil.

When a recipe in this book lists 'oil', I have used either **canola** or olive oil, and sometimes both. The former comes from rape seed, has a particularly low saturated fat level, and is lower in price than olive oil, but the latter has become an essential ingredient in pantries world-wide. It is high in mono-unsaturated fat, with anti-oxidant properties and a matchless flavour. Trouble is, there's so much hype about which to buy: extra virgin, cold-pressed, pure, refined, blended... Some are best reserved for dressing salads, some are best used in cooking. The colours differ, the flavours differ, and the only way to find out which you prefer is to try them all and then follow your preference, bearing in mind that oils vary from one producer to another and can also have seasonal variations. Extra virgin, the greenish one which comes from the first pressing, is the one strongly punted by many food writers these days. Pure, unrefined and low in acidity, but the flavour can be too intense for some palates, and in most of my recipes I have used a mild and light blend of refined and **virgin oil**, which is versatile, being bland rather than fruity. That said, all that remains is for you to collect your pasta and the other ingredients – mostly fresh and simple – that play the major role in Italian cuisine.

pasta

Vegetable Bake with Pasta and Herbs

Bake a tumble of **vegetables** in **olive oil** and **wine**, stir in some **pasta** and **fresh herbs**, top with **feta cheese** and relish the pot-pourri of flavours and shapes in this one-dish meal. The vegetables can be prepared in advance, leaving only the pasta requiring last-minute attention.

4 medium carrots
  (250 g/9 oz), julienned
3 large tomatoes
  (400 g/14 oz), chopped
200 g (7 oz) green beans,
  trimmed and sliced
6 baby marrows (200 g/7 oz), pared
  and julienned (prepared weight)
2 sticks table celery, plus some
  leaves, chopped
3 slim leeks, thinly sliced
1 large red pepper, seeded and diced
75 ml (5 tbsp) olive oil
75 ml (5 tbsp) white wine
5 ml (1 tsp) salt
a pinch of sugar
2–3 cloves garlic, crushed
2 bay leaves
250 g (9 oz) elbow macaroni
30–45 ml (2–3 tbsp) chopped fresh
  herbs*
feta cheese, crumbled

Place all the prepared vegetables in a large baking dish, not a roasting tin, (about 27 x 22 x 6 cm/11 x 8¾ x 2¼ in). Mix the oil, wine, salt, sugar and garlic, pour over the vegetables and toss to mix. Tuck in the bay leaves, and, if working ahead, cover securely and set aside. Cover and bake at 180 °C (350 °F, Gas Mark 4) for 30–35 minutes, until just tender. Meanwhile, cook the pasta and drain well. Stir into the vegetables together with the herbs, top with plenty of feta and return to the oven for 10 minutes or until piping hot.

SERVES 6.

* Use whatever grows in your garden. Failing that, your neighbour's garden. Failing that, use the fresh herbs you can buy at some supermarkets. Best suited to this dish are origanum, thyme, basil, marjoram and a touch of parsley.

Fusilli with Vegetables, Gremolata and Feta

A mixture of *parsley*, *garlic* and *lemon rind* (gremolata) adds delicious piquancy to this brilliant *pasta bake* of juicy *vegetables* and colourful *fusilli*, under a blanket of crumbled *feta cheese*. Once the vegetables have been prepared, further attention is minimal, and the result is a really hearty dish to serve with crusty *Italian bread* and a *salad*.

250 g (9 oz) young brinjals*, cubed
400 g (14 oz) tomatoes, chopped
250 g (9 oz) white mushrooms,
   wiped, halved if large
250 g (9 oz) baby marrows, pared
   and sliced (prepared weight)
2 medium leeks, sliced
2 stalks table celery, sliced
1 large red pepper, seeded
   and slivered

DRESSING
125 ml (4½ fl oz) olive oil
30 ml (2 tbsp) lemon juice
2 cloves garlic, crushed
7 ml (1½ tsp) dried origanum
5 ml (1 tsp) salt
10 ml (2 tsp) honey

GREMOLATA
a handful of parsley, finely
   chopped
2 cloves garlic, crushed
5 ml (1 tsp) finely grated
   lemon rind

250 g (9 oz) fusilli tri-colore
300–400 g (11–14 oz) feta cheese,
   crumbled

Place all the vegetables in a large, deep baking dish (about

22 x 27 cm/8¾ x 11 in). (A Corningware roaster is just right.) Mix

the ingredients for the dressing, toss with the vegetables, cover

and stand for 1–2 hours. Uncover and bake at 200 °C (400 °F, Gas

Mark 6) for 15 minutes, toss to mix in the juices that will have

started to run, then bake for a further 15 minutes or until cooked

but not mushy. Meanwhile cook the fusilli and drain. Fork the

pasta into the vegetables, together with the gremolata, top with

feta and return to the oven for 15 minutes until bubbling.

SERVES 8.

* If using 1 medium to large brinjal, it is best dégorged (see p. 161).

Polly se Pasta

The best seafood pasta I have ever eaten was in a small village on the west coast of Scotland. Our waitress was a bonny wee lass with an accent which I couldn't quite place, so I asked her whether she hailed from the Highlands or the Hebrides. 'Stellenbosch, actually,' came the reply.

It's true. Because the rivers and seas in Scotland bristle with salmon, crabs, scallops, oysters and mussels, Polly se Pasta is naturally much simpler, here, than there. Nevertheless it's a fairly pricey dish, but very good and hugely satisfying.

45 ml (3 tbsp) oil

15 ml (1 tbsp) butter

2 large leeks, finely chopped

1 small onion, chopped

300 g (11 oz) calamari, sliced into
small, thin rings, well dried*

30 ml (2 tbsp) whisky, warmed

250 g (9 oz) white mushrooms,
wiped and sliced

1 x 410 g (14 oz) can tomatoes,
chopped, plus juice

15 ml (1 tbsp) tomato paste
(see p. 208)

125 ml (4½ fl oz) fish or
chicken stock

45 ml (3 tbsp) chopped parsley

a little salt

10 ml (2 tsp) sugar

4 bay leaves

4 large sprigs fresh thyme
or lemon thyme

200 g (7 oz) filleted kingklip,
cut into very small cubes
(see p. 208)

100 g (3½ oz) cooked shrimps

300–400 g (11–14 oz) spaghetti
or linguine

Heat the oil and butter in a large, deep, heavy saucepan (not a frying pan), add the leeks and onion and, when softening, add the calamari. Toss until the calamari stiffens and turns white, then flame with the whisky – stand well back! (Even if doubling up on quantities, don't double the whisky, it flames like a bush fire.) Shake the pan until the flames die down, then add the remaining ingredients, except the kingklip and shrimps. Reduce heat, cover tightly and simmer, popping very gently, for about 45 minutes. Check once or twice to see that it is not boiling rapidly, and give it a quick stir at the same time. When an exquisite aroma fills the kitchen, you'll know that the calamari is done to a turn in a brilliant, medium-thick sauce. Now slip in the kingklip and shrimps and continue to simmer, uncovered, for about 10 minutes – you can fish out the bay leaves and thyme stalks and cook the pasta at the same time. If the sauce is too thick, add a little extra stock; if too thin, drop in a pat of beurre manié – 15 ml (1 tbsp) butter mashed with 15 ml (1 tbsp) flour. Check seasoning – I sometimes add a dash of lemon juice here to highlight the flavour. To serve, ladle the pasta into big bowls and top with sauce – you're not supposed to serve this with Parmesan, but I do, and it's great.

SERVES 6.

* You can use calamari rings, tubes or steaks cut into thin strips. For the correct amount you must weigh it after thawing, so buy a bit more than the 300 g (11 oz) specified.

Pasta-pesto Salad with Fresh and Sun-dried Tomatoes

A simple but spectacular flavour-of-the-month **salad** to serve at a Mediterranean-style buffet, with **focaccia** and carafes of red wine. To make it even more substantial and delicious, toss in some **mussels** before serving.

DRESSING

60 ml (4 tbsp) olive oil
60 ml (4 tbsp) sunflower oil
30 ml (2 tbsp) lemon juice
2 cloves garlic, crushed
a pinch each of salt and sugar
30–45 ml (2–3 tbsp) basil pesto

SALAD

sun-dried tomatoes in oil
250 g (9 oz) fusilli tri-colore
  or elbow macaroni
4 medium tomatoes, diced
1 bunch spring onions, chopped
500 ml (60 g/2 oz) spinach,
  finely shredded
250 g (9 oz) feta cheese,
  preferably herbed, diced
fresh basil and Throubes olives
  to garnish*

First mix all the ingredients for the dressing, then set aside. Drain the sun-dried tomatoes and snip into slivers – you will need about 125 ml (60 g/2 oz). Cook the pasta, drain well, tip into a large, shallow salad platter and immediately toss with dressing. Add the remaining ingredients, except the feta, cool, cover loosely with a kitchen towel and let it stand for an hour or two to develop the flavours. Just before serving, fork in the feta and check seasoning – it will probably need salt and a grind of pepper. If using mussels, add one or two 250 g (9 oz) cans mussels in brine, rinsed and drained. Scatter with basil and olives.

SERVES 6–8.

* These are super little wrinkly olives, but any black olives may be substituted.

Pink Salmon and Noodle Bake

Pasta *al dente* tangled with fine, fresh ingredients is all very good and proper, but there are times when a pre-prepared, **saucy casserole** is more practical. This is a good one.

30 ml (2 tbsp) each butter and oil*
75 ml (5 tbsp) flour
5 ml (1 tsp) mustard powder
600 ml (1 pint) hot milk**
salt and white pepper
5 ml (1 tsp) Worcestershire sauce
250 ml (100 g/3½ oz) grated
   Cheddar cheese
20 ml (4 tsp) anchovy paste
1 x 415 g (15 oz) can pink salmon,
   drained
250 g (9 oz) spinach noodles
2–3 large tomatoes, sliced
mixed dried Italian herbs
30–45 ml (2–3 tbsp) grated
   Parmesan cheese

Melt the butter and oil, add the flour and mustard, simmer until straw-coloured and bubbling, then slowly add the milk, stirring all the while (use a balloon whisk if you have one). Keep the heat low and stir until the sauce thickens. Remove from the stove, then add the seasoning, Worcestershire sauce, cheese and anchovy paste. When the cheese has melted, add the salmon – skin, dark flesh and bones removed, and flaked. Cook the noodles and drain very well. Lightly oil a deep, 21 cm (8¼ in) square dish and spread one-third of the sauce over the base. Top with half the noodles, cover with half the tomatoes, sprinkle lightly with herbs, then repeat layers, ending with a layer of sauce. Sprinkle Parmesan over the top. Set aside briefly at this stage if working ahead. Bake, uncovered, at 180 °C (350 °F, Gas Mark 4) for 30 minutes. Serve with Italian bread and a green salad.
SERVES 6.

* In these days of cutting fats, it has become perfectly acceptable to substitute oil for some of the butter in a white sauce.
** Half full cream milk, half low-fat may be used.

Pasta, Stuffed Mushrooms and Fresh Tomato Sauce

Sparkling with new flavours, tints and textures, this is a joyful departure from pasta with pesto, pasta with bolognese, pasta whatever. The trio is  not complicated to prepare, but the combination is novel and attractive: a tangle of *pasta*, a topping of *mushrooms*, and a vivid *tomato sauce* with which to lavish each serving.

Pasta, Stuffed Mushrooms and Fresh Tomato Sauce

20–24 medium brown mushrooms
(about 800 g/1¾ lb) wiped

30 ml (2 tbsp) each oil and butter

1 large onion, finely chopped

4 cloves garlic, crushed

1 large red pepper, seeded
and diced

4 x 250 ml (120 g/4 oz) shredded
spinach leaves

10 ml (2 tsp) chopped fresh
rosemary leaves

5 ml (1 tsp) salt

250 g (9 oz) Ricotta cheese

Parmesan cheese, freshly grated

500 g (1 lb 2 oz) thin pasta
(spaghetti, tagliarini or
vermicelli)

FRESH TOMATO SAUCE

1 kg (2¼ lb) tomatoes, skinned
and chopped

1 large onion, chopped

5 ml (1 tsp) each salt and sugar

a handful of fresh basil leaves

30 ml (2 tbsp) tomato paste
(see p. 208)

a small knob of butter

Remove mushroom stems together with a little flesh and chop these trimmings. Heat the oil and butter and add the trimmings together with the remaining ingredients, except the cheeses and pasta. Toss constantly over low heat for about 5 minutes, until the spinach is limp and the mixture reduced. Remove from heat and stir in the Ricotta. If working ahead, set aside at this stage. Arrange the mushrooms, hollows facing up, in two large baking dishes, bases lightly oiled. Spoon in the stuffing, sprinkle lightly with the Parmesan cheese and bake at 180 °C (350 °F, Gas Mark 4) for about 25 minutes, until softened but not shrivelled. To make the sauce, place all the ingredients in a processor or blender, and purée. Pour into a saucepan and simmer, uncovered, until reduced, thickened and a rich, ripe red. Meanwhile, cook the pasta. Serve mushrooms on individual portions of hot pasta, allowing three or four per diner, and pass the sauce separately.

SERVES 5–6.

Chicken Liver, Mushroom and Bacon Pasta

Cavatappi are small, wriggly **pasta spirals**, and are just the right shape to coat with this **rich brown sauce**. The Italians, however, have invented hundreds of different ribbons and bows, tubes, shells and twisty pastas, so it shouldn't be difficult to find another wriggle if cavatappi is not available.

250 g (9 oz) chicken livers

30 ml (2 tbsp) olive oil

1 large onion, finely chopped

2–3 rashers lean bacon, chopped

2 cloves garlic, crushed

2 bay leaves

125 g (4½ oz) brown mushrooms, wiped and chopped

1 ml (¼ tsp) grated nutmeg

30 ml (2 tbsp) sweet sherry

125 ml (4½ fl oz) tomato purée (see p. 208)

250 ml (9 fl oz) hot chicken stock

a little salt and sugar to taste

Tabasco

250 g (9 oz) cavatappi spirals

finely chopped parsley to garnish

Trim livers, discarding any greenish-white bits. (Actually, your friendly butcher should have done this already.) Rinse them in vinegar-water, pat dry and slice. Heat the oil in a fairly large frying pan, add the onion, bacon and garlic and cook until the bacon is crisp and the onion lightly browned. Remove from the pan and set aside. Reduce heat and add the livers and bay leaves to the pan, toss until no longer pink, then add the mushrooms, nutmeg and sherry. As soon as the sherry has boiled away, add the tomato purée, stock, reserved onion-bacon mixture and seasoning, except the Tabasco. Simmer for about 5 minutes, stirring gently, until the sauce thickens, then toss with freshly cooked pasta, adding a few drops of Tabasco. Serve sprinkled with parsley and pass a green salad.

SERVES 4.

Three Quick ways with Pasta

1. A Trio of Mushrooms and Mascarpone

Seriously **sumptuous** and expensive.

500 g (1 lb 2 oz) mixed mushrooms
  (white, brown and oyster)
60 ml (4 tbsp) olive oil
1 bunch spring onions, chopped
4 cloves garlic, crushed
5 ml (1 tsp) finely grated
  lemon rind
2 sprigs fresh rosemary
250 ml (9 fl oz) hot chicken stock
60 ml (4 tbsp) red wine
125 g (4½ oz) mascarpone cheese
salt and milled black pepper
300 g (11 oz) spaghetti or linguine
60 ml (4 tbsp) grated
  Parmesan cheese

Clean and slice all the mushrooms. Heat the oil, add the onions, garlic and lemon rind, toss for 1 minute, then add the mushrooms and rosemary. Cook over low heat for 1–2 minutes until the mushrooms start to shrink, then add the stock and wine. Simmer until the liquid reduces and becomes syrupy, remove the rosemary and add the mascarpone and seasoning. Continue to cook gently, stirring, until the sauce reduces again and thickens. Meanwhile cook the pasta, drain (reserve water) and return it to its saucepan. Slowly add 60 ml (4 tbsp) of the cooking water and, when absorbed, add the mushroom sauce and Parmesan and toss to combine. Serve with extra Parmesan, if you wish.

SERVES 6.

2. Garlic and Fresh Herbs
The **purest** and most **wholesome** of them all.

60 ml (4 tbsp) olive oil

3 plump cloves garlic, chopped
with a pinch of salt

6–8 spring onions, plus some
green tops, chopped

250 g (9 oz) whole-wheat
pasta spirals

250 ml (22 g/¾ oz) finely
chopped parsley

fresh herbs, finely chopped*

45 ml (3 tbsp) grated
Parmesan cheese

about 12 black olives, stoned
and slivered

salt and milled black pepper

Heat the oil in a small saucepan, add the garlic and onions and simmer for a few minutes until aromatic. Set aside. Cook the pasta, drain in a colander set over a bowl, then return the pasta to the saucepan in which it was cooked. Slowly add 60 ml (4 tbsp) of the cooking water to the pasta, 15 ml (1 tbsp) at a time, allowing each to be absorbed before adding the next. Add the garlic-onion oil, then the remaining ingredients. Toss everything together for about 2 minutes until very hot and fragrant, and serve immediately with hot Italian bread, a bowl of finely chopped tomatoes, and extra Parmesan if desired.

SERVES 4.

* I use marjoram, lemon thyme and basil leaves, a smidgin of rosemary, and chives or garlic chives. Use enough to fill half a large cup.

3. Lisa's Walnut and Spinach Pasta

Pretty rich, but so **delectable**.

75 g (2½ oz) walnuts

2 cloves garlic, chopped

30 ml (2 tbsp) soft butter

a handful of parsley tufts

3 slim spring onions, chopped

60 ml (4 tbsp) olive oil

30 ml (2 tbsp) grated
   Parmesan cheese

2 ml (½ tsp) salt

250 g (9 oz) spaghetti or
   spaghettini

4 x 250 ml (120 g/4 oz) shredded
   English spinach leaves

2 ml (½ tsp) grated nutmeg

Roast walnuts in a moderate oven for about 10 minutes, or dry-roast in a non-stick frying pan until lightly browned. Rub gently in a clean kitchen towel to remove loose skins, then chop roughly and place in a processor fitted with the metal blade. Add the garlic, butter, parsley, onions, oil, cheese and salt, then pulse – do not over-process as the mixture must be a bit chunky. Scrape into a bowl. Cook the pasta, and tip into a colander set over a bowl to retain the cooking water. Return the pasta, which should still be a little moist, to its saucepan, add the spinach and nutmeg and toss briefly until the spinach starts to wilt. Quickly mix 60 ml (4 tbsp) of the reserved water into the nut mixture, add it to the pasta, and toss until combined and piping hot. Serve on heated plates with extra Parmesan, if desired.

SERVES 4.

Garlicky Fettucine with Vegetables

Softly simmered **vegetables** touched with **herbs** and creamed with **garlic** butter, this succulent sauce could easily become a busy cook's favourite accompaniment to **pasta**. Almost as easy to prepare as a basic Neapolitan sauce, but with a far finer edge to the flavour.

30 ml (2 tbsp) olive oil
1 medium onion, chopped
1 large yellow pepper, seeded
  and diced
250 g (9 oz) baby marrows, pared
  and sliced (prepared weight)
200 g (7 oz) white mushrooms,
  wiped and sliced
5 ml (1 tsp) dried tarragon
2 ml (½ tsp) dried dill
1 x 410 g (14 oz) can tomatoes,
  chopped, plus juice
90 ml (6 tbsp) chopped parsley
a little salt
5 ml (1 tsp) sugar
60 ml (4 tbsp) white wine
60 ml (4 tbsp) water
15 ml (1 tbsp) soft butter
3 cloves garlic, crushed
15 ml (1 tbsp) flour
250–300 g (9–11 oz) fettucine,
  cooked and well drained*

Heat the oil, together with the onion, yellow pepper, marrows, mushrooms and herbs in a large frying pan. Stir to mix, then cover and sweat over very low heat, tossing once or twice until softening, aromatic and starting to draw juices – about 10 minutes. Stir in the tomatoes, parsley, salt, sugar, wine and water, then cover and simmer for a further 10 minutes or until the vegetables are cooked and the mixture is very succulent. Mash the butter to a paste with the garlic and flour and add small pats to the pan, stirring until thickened. Ladle the sauce over servings of cooked pasta. Serve with grated Parmesan cheese for sprinkling, a dressed salad and warm ciabatta.
SERVES 4.

* Toss the fettucine with 15 ml (1 tbsp) each olive oil and poppy seeds before serving, to brighten up those squiggles a bit.

Creamy Pasta Salad with Smoked Salmon and Mushrooms

A beautiful salad, with the natural flavours of *lemon* and *fresh dill* highlighting the salmon just perfectly. Use *salmon* off-cuts rather than thin slices – not only are they cheaper, but being thicker they add the right chunky texture. For the best flavour, assemble and refrigerate for several hours or overnight. Serve on a bed of bright *lettuce leaves*, with chunks of hot *Continental bread*.

250 g (9 oz) fusilli, preferably
  tri-colore
250 g (9 oz) white mushrooms,
  wiped with a paper towel soaked
  in lemon juice, then thinly sliced
a few spring onions, chopped
60 ml (4 tbsp) chopped parsley
60 ml (4 tbsp) lemon juice
60 ml (4 tbsp) olive oil
60 ml (4 tbsp) mayonnaise
15 ml (1 tbsp) Dijon mustard
60 ml (4 tbsp) cultured sour cream
250 g (9 oz) smoked salmon,
  roughly slivered
60 ml (4 tbsp) chopped fresh dill*
salt, black pepper and a little sugar
fresh dill and capers and
  something bright, like
  nasturtiums, to garnish

Cook the pasta, drain well and tip into a large bowl. Immediately add the mushrooms, onions, parsley, lemon juice and oil. Toss to mix, then cool until no longer steaming. Mix the mayonnaise, mustard and sour cream and fold in. Add the salmon, dill and seasoning and mix in lightly. Spoon the mixture into a large refrigerator container and chill. Happily, you should taste this salad before serving, because the pasta and mushrooms absorb a lot of the dressing. You might want to add another splosh of oil, or an extra dash of lemon juice, and/or salt, pepper, a pinch of sugar and extra dill. It's tempting to go on tasting, but remember you have guests to feed. Pile lightly onto a big platter and garnish.

SERVES 8.

* Dill is a great herb to plant in your patch. You can use it, they say, to ward off both indigestion and witchcraft, which is useful. But it's an annual herb, and when not available I have substituted about 30 ml (2 tbsp) fresh lemon thyme leaves. In this case, go easy on the lemon juice.

Spinach Pasta with Brinjals and Tomato-Red Wine Sauce

This homespun dish incorporates some of the finest Mediterranean flavours. The ingredients are **fresh**, the colour **good**, the flavour **bold**, and the strands of **melting cheese** provide the ultimate slurp.

45 ml (3 tbsp) olive oil

1 large onion, finely chopped

3 small brinjals (400–500 g/ 14 oz–1 lb 2 oz), cut into small cubes, dégorged, rinsed and dried

500 g (1 lb 2 oz) ripe, juicy tomatoes, skinned and chopped*

15 ml (1 tbsp) tomato paste (see p. 208)

60 ml (4 tbsp) red wine

250 ml (9 fl oz) vegetable stock

60 ml (4 tbsp) chopped parsley

a little salt and sugar to taste

3 cloves garlic, crushed

200 g (7 oz) Mozzarella cheese, diced

45 ml (3 tbsp) fresh basil leaves, torn

300 g (11 oz) spinach ribbon noodles

roasted pine nuts

Heat the oil in a large, wide-based frying pan, add the onion and, when softened, add the brinjals. Toss until glistening, then add the remaining ingredients, except the garlic, cheese and basil. Cover and simmer gently, stirring occasionally, until the brinjals are cooked but still chunky and the tomatoes 'melted' – about 25 minutes. The sauce should be medium-thick – if necessary add a little more stock. Stir in the garlic and cheese and, when melting, swirl in the basil. Moisten the freshly cooked pasta with a ladleful of the water in which it was cooked, and serve with the sauce. Pass the nuts separately. This dish is so filling, just a salad will complete the meal.

SERVES 4–6.

* Use fresh, not canned tomatoes for this dish.

Oriental Pasta Salad with Spicy Chicken Nuggets

Whether Marco Polo introduced pasta to Italy after

visiting the Orient is debatable – some say he

returned with noodles in his saddlebag, while others

say the Etruscans were eating pasta long before he was born. The

fact remains that pasta and *Oriental flavours* have a wonderful

affinity for each other, as proved by this jumbo salad.

Oriental Pasta Salad with Spicy Chicken Nuggets

CHICKEN
600 g (1¼ lb) skinless
  chicken breast fillets
2 cloves garlic, crushed
30 ml (2 tbsp) oil
30 ml (2 tbsp) soy sauce
30 ml (2 tbsp) lemon juice
2 ml (½ tsp) Chinese Five-Spice
5 ml (1 tsp) ground ginger
10 ml (2 tsp) soft brown sugar

DRESSING
300 ml (11 fl oz) oil
125 ml (4½ fl oz) lemon juice
60 ml (4 tbsp) soy sauce
10 ml (2 tsp) honey
3 cloves garlic, crushed
60 ml (4 tbsp) toasted sesame seeds
60 ml (4 tbsp) chopped fresh
  coriander leaves
45 ml (3 tbsp) lemon grass,
  chopped OR some finely grated
  lemon rind

SALAD
500 g (1 lb 2 oz) fusilli tri-colore
250 g (9 oz) white mushrooms,
  wiped and thinly sliced
4 sticks table celery, thinly sliced
a bunch of spring onions, chopped
a handful of chopped parsley

extra toasted sesame seeds to
  garnish

Slice the chicken into strips across the grain, then into small chunks. Place in a large, shallow glass or other non-metallic dish. Add all the remaining ingredients and toss until well mixed, then leave to marinate for 30 minutes. Heat a large heavy pan, add the chicken, reduce heat and toss until cooked through (no pink insides). If working ahead, cool and refrigerate.

If using lemon grass, use fleshy part of the stems, bruised, and outer layer removed. Mix all the ingredients in a screw-top jar, shake well and set aside.

Cook the pasta, drain well, then tip into a large salad bowl and add the dressing immediately, while still steaming. Fork in the remaining ingredients, toss until well mixed, allow to cool, then cover loosely. Leave to stand for a while to allow the flavours to develop, then mix in the chicken and check seasoning – it may need extra soy sauce. Sprinkle generously with sesame seeds and serve immediately.

SERVES 10–12.

vegetarian dishes & grains

One evening I was taken to dinner at a famous seafood restaurant on Sydney harbour. Unfortunately I had just returned from a brilliant snorkelling trip on the Barrier reef, and the memory of those luminous fish in that underwater world was still very fresh in my mind. Too fresh for me to eat a sea creature right then. So I asked the waiter for anything **vegetarian**. This upset a very fat man at the adjoining table. He leaned over and said to his wife, loudly so that I could hear, 'Never liked vegetarians, myself. Funny people. Pinch blankets on airplanes. Have cats called Muffin. Lark about.' He cracked a lobster claw with his teeth. 'Don't understand 'em, never liked 'em.' I smiled into my **spinach quiche**. 'Nuts to you,' I muttered, acknowledging the strange, sad fact that those who don't enjoy vegetarian meals often scorn those who do.

This is a pity because I think they're absolutely great. We have them on a regular basis – probably more often than meat, fish or fowl. And I'm not talking **baked potatoes** here. I'm talking low-fat, high protein **beans and pulses** which, combined with fibre-rich grains and vegetables, make a balanced meal. A further bonus is the absence of the additives often found in processed foods.

There was a time when busy cooks could quite honestly say that **meatless meals** took too long to prepare, what with all that overnight soaking and rinsing and boiling and chopping. True, this used to be daunting, but it is possible these days to buy most items in cans – beans in abundance, **chickpeas**, **lentils**, **sprouts** ... not the same as home-prepared, but jolly useful nevertheless. One can also buy ready-washed **salads**. And organically grown **greens**. They cost a bit more, but it's nice to know that your leaves have soaked up rainwater and not pesticides.

Whether we're eating vegetarian or 'regular', I always have a fresh salad on the table. Add a vegetable **curry**, some pasta with herbs, chickpeas with bulgur, or butternuts with stuffing, and I reckon it will take a very narrow-minded palate not to be tempted.

PS I don't have a cat called Muffin. I don't have a cat at all, but if I did, that's probably what I'd call it.

vegetarian
dishes & grains

Stuffed Mushrooms with Nutty Rice and Lentils

Of the dozens of stuffings for baked brown **mushrooms**, a combination of cream **cheese** and fresh **spinach** is surely one of the simplest and best. In this recipe, the plumped mushrooms are nestled on a bed of **tomato** slices, blanketed with cheese, baked and served on a mixture of grains and legumes.

500 g (1 lb 2 oz) large brown
   mushrooms
30 ml (2 tbsp) each oil and butter
1 medium onion, finely chopped
4 x 250 ml (120 g/4 oz) shredded
   spinach leaves
2 ml (½ tsp) grated nutmeg
125 ml (100–120 g/3½–4 oz)
   cream cheese*
60 ml (4 tbsp) finely chopped parsley
3 cloves garlic, crushed
salt and milled black pepper
tomatoes, sliced into large rings
extra salt and a little sugar
dried origanum
crumbled feta cheese or
   sliced Mozzarella
paprika

Wipe the mushrooms and, using a grapefruit spoon, scoop out the stems and a little of the flesh to enlarge the hollows. Heat the oil and butter and sauté the onion and chopped mushroom stems. Add the spinach and nutmeg and toss over low heat until cooked and dry. Spoon into a bowl, cool slightly, then slowly mix in the cheese, parsley, garlic and seasoning. Lightly oil a baking dish in which the mushrooms will fit fairly snugly, and line with tomato slices – one for each mushroom. Sprinkle the tomatoes with a little salt, sugar and origanum, top with mushrooms, hollows facing up, and spread with stuffing. Cover the mushrooms with cheese, dust with paprika and bake at 180 ˚C (350 ˚F, Gas Mark 4) for 25–30 minutes. (If working ahead, cover with cling wrap and refrigerate, but return to room temperature before baking.) Serve with a mixture of cooked brown rice and lentils, tossed while hot with chopped parsley, sunflower seeds, diced red pepper and a little butter to moisten.
SERVES 4–6.

* Low-fat, smooth cottage cheese (see p. 208) can be substituted.

Linda's Health Salad

A recipe for a nutritious, **grainy salad** to eat at her desk was a request from my editor, and a request from an editor is simply a euphemism for 'Do it'. So who am I to argue?

DRESSING
125 ml (4½ fl oz) oil
30 ml (2 tbsp) soy sauce
45 ml (3 tbsp) lemon juice
30 ml (2 tbsp) honey
1 clove garlic, crushed

SALAD
250 ml (200 g/7 oz) stampkoring
   (pearled whole wheat), rinsed*
200 ml (160 g/5½ oz) brown
   lentils, rinsed
60 ml (4 tbsp) seedless raisins
1 large red pepper, seeded
   and diced
6–8 slim spring onions, chopped
100 ml (50 g/1¾ oz) toasted
   sunflower seeds
a handful of chopped parsley
250 ml (30 g/1 oz) finely shredded
   spinach

Mix all the ingredients for the dressing and set aside. Soak the stampkoring in cold water for 2 hours, drain and boil, covered, in 750 ml (1¼ pints) salted water for about 35 minutes, until tender and the water has been absorbed. In a separate pan, boil the lentils in 450 ml (16 fl oz) salted water for about 40 minutes until soft – drain if necessary. In both cases, before cooking, cover the bases of the saucepans with a slick of oil to prevent catching, and do not stir while cooking. When done, tip both steaming grains into a large bowl, immediately fork in the dressing, add the remaining salad ingredients and toss lightly to mix. Cool, then cover loosely. To store, spoon into a glass bowl, cover and refrigerate until the next day before taking it to the office.

SERVES 6 (EDITORS).

* Stampkoring, also known as weet-rice or pearled whole wheat, does not necessarily have to be soaked beforehand, but this does shorten the cooking time. If you want it fluffier, steam it in a colander once cooked. Watch it closely – if it boils dry, it will burn in a flash.

Stuffed Butternut Squash

If you've ever tried baking a raw, **stuffed butternut**, you'll know that it takes until tomorrow to soften, so in this dish everything is first cooked and assembled, then baked. These buxom **butternuts** make a filling, low-cost meal, with **chickpeas** adding a dollop of protein, but you could substitute **brown rice** with a topping of grated **cheese** if preferred.

2 butternuts (long and cylindrical
   rather than bulbous,
   600–700 g/1¼–1½ lb each)
warmed honey
15 ml (1 tbsp) each oil and butter
1 medium onion, finely chopped
2 cloves garlic, crushed
5 ml (1 tsp) each ground cumin,
   coriander and ginger
1 x 400 g (14 oz) can chickpeas,
   drained
60 ml (4 tbsp) sunflower seeds
60 ml (4 tbsp) currants
2 medium tomatoes, skinned
   and chopped
15 ml (1 tbsp) soy sauce
Greek yoghurt or cultured
   sour cream and ground
   cinnamon for the topping

Scrub the butternuts, halve them lengthways and place, cut sides down, in a large saucepan (if you don't have one that will take them in a single layer, use a baking dish) and bake at 180 °C (350 °F, Gas Mark 4). In either case, the butternuts should be cooked in a little salted water until soft, but not wrinkled – test by piercing with a skewer. Cool in the cooking liquid, then discard the pips and scoop out most of the flesh, leaving a firm shell. Place skin side down in a baking dish, brush the hollows lightly with honey, and pour a little water in at the side. To make the stuffing, heat the oil and butter, add the onion, garlic and spices, and toss until the onion softens. Add the remaining ingredients and the butternut flesh. Mix well, then pile into shells, drizzle with yoghurt or sour cream, sprinkle with cinnamon and bake at 180 °C (350 °F, Gas Mark 4) for 30 minutes. SERVES 4.

Double Mushroom and Red Wine Risotto

When I recall that the best Italian risotto I have ever eaten was in a French restaurant in London, it becomes clear that dining out can, geographically speaking, be something of a bewilderment. I mean, if you can get home-made hummus in the Hebrides (and that's a fact), perfect polenta in Pretoria, and flawless Italian in French in England, anything becomes possible. I call it global food confusion, and it has come about because so many national ingredients are now internationally available. Given the basic items, any cook can copy any cuisine back home in her kitchen and this means that, with a packet of arborio rice, anyone, anywhere, can make risotto. This is a favourite version – I wouldn't call it classic, but it's jolly nice: a combination of *meaty oyster* and *brown mushrooms*, with a touch of *red wine* and a whiff of *nutmeg* adding a glorious flavour. *Arborio rice* is positively the only one to use – the grains are short, round, and able to absorb a lot of liquid without becoming sticky, and the result should be a creamy and moist delight. It will, however, be a disaster if you don't pay it constant attention. With risotto, you absolutely have to stick around.

45 ml (3 tbsp) butter

15 ml (1 tbsp) olive oil

1 medium onion, finely chopped

2–3 cloves garlic, crushed

125 g (4½ oz) oyster mushrooms,
  sliced

125 g (4½ oz) brown mushrooms,
  wiped and thinly sliced

375 ml (300 g/11 oz) arborio rice

2 ml (½ tsp) grated nutmeg

125 ml (4½ fl oz) red wine

1 litre (1¾ pints) hot vegetable
  stock

a little salt and pepper

30 ml (2 tbsp) grated
  Parmesan cheese

extra butter or olive oil

thinly shaved Parmesan or
  Ricotelo cheese and chopped
  parsley to garnish

Heat the butter and oil in a deep, wide (about 24 cm/9½ in diameter) frying pan and lightly sauté the onion and garlic. Add all the mushrooms and toss for a minute until they start to shrink. Stir in the rice, toss until coated, then mix in the nutmeg and add the wine. Stir lightly until absorbed, then add 250 ml (9 fl oz) of the hot stock. Simmer very gently until absorbed, stirring so that it doesn't stick to the bottom of the pan. Add the remaining stock in small doses – about 200 ml (7 fl oz) at a time, waiting for each dose to be absorbed before adding the next. Continue until all the stock has been used – this should take 25–30 minutes. When done, the rice should be tender and creamy, but still with a nuttiness to the bite – you might have to add a little extra stock and add on 5 minutes cooking time. Season, then stir in the Parmesan and a little extra butter or oil. Garnish and serve.

SERVES 4–6.

Layered Mediterranean Vegetable and Cheese Bake

I first met this dish on a soft summer's evening in Cape Town. I had chosen to dine at a small bistro-type place because the owner had set a few tables out on the pavement, which meant that I could sit in full view of the heart-stopping bulk of Table Mountain. I sat and gazed at it for so long that a passing waiter stopped and, resting his tray on my table, looked intently into my face and asked me if I was awake. I turned my head, and it was love at first sight: *glossy brinjals*, a ripple of *red tomatoes*, a whiff of *herbs* and an eiderdown of *cheese*, all steaming together in a little earthenware bowl. Back home I fiddled a bit in my kitchen and turned up this slightly different version of Italian Brinjal Pie. Like the authentic Parmigiana Di Melanzane, it's such a merry dish. Perhaps it's the warm Italian temperament that flavours it; perhaps it's the red wine (and lots of herbed focaccia) that accompanies it. Or perhaps it's the fact that this type of food is very popular at present, and it's comforting to know that your guests will enjoy it – particularly if they're young and vegetarian. But this is not necessary. I serve it to all ages and find it has just the right ingredients (inexpensive, do-ahead, filling) for casual party food.

1–1.2 kg (2¼–2¾ lb) brinjals, sliced no more than 1 cm (⅜ in) thick, dégorged

olive oil

2 large onions, finely chopped

2 x 410 g (14 oz) cans tomatoes, chopped, plus juice

400 g (14 oz) baby marrows, pared and sliced (prepared weight)

10 ml (2 tsp) dried Italian herbs

4 cloves garlic, crushed

30 ml (2 tbsp) tomato paste (see p. 208)

15 ml (1 tbsp) sugar

a little salt

125 ml (4½ fl oz) white wine

a handful of chopped parsley

400 g (14 oz) Mozzarella cheese, thinly sliced

60 ml (4 tbsp) grated Parmesan cheese

Once dégorged (salt, weight with a heavy pot, leave to sweat for 45 minutes, rinse and dry well), place the brinjals in a single layer on two baking trays (line them with baking paper for easy cleaning afterwards) and brush with olive oil. Turn the slices, brush again, then bake at 200 °C (400 °F, Gas Mark 6) for 25–30 minutes until soft and starting to brown. If they look oily, drain on paper towels. While the brinjals are baking, heat an extra 60 ml (4 tbsp) olive oil in a large frying pan, add the onions and, when softened, add the remaining ingredients, except the cheeses. Mix everything well, then cover and simmer gently for about 30 minutes, stirring occasionally, until the marrows are soft. (You may have to uncover the pan for the last 5 minutes to achieve the right texture – the sauce should be thick, but not dry.) Arrange half the brinjal slices in a large, lightly oiled baking dish – cover the base completely. Spread over half the tomato sauce, cover with half the Mozzarella and sprinkle with half the Parmesan. Repeat layers. Bake uncovered at 180 °C (350 °F, Gas Mark 4) for 30–35 minutes until piping hot and the cheese has melted.

SERVES 8–10.

* Make and assemble the entire dish in the afternoon if you like, and bake when required.

Almond Rice and Lentil Pilaff with Yoghurt Raita

This is an extraordinarily addictive **pilaff**, so be prepared for second helpings. It's **colourful**, **spicy** and warming and, served with a ribbon of the fragrant **raita** at the side, shredded **omelette** on the top and a dressed **green salad**, it makes a wholesome, complete meal.

YOGHURT RAITA (MAKE THIS A FEW HOURS IN ADVANCE)

10 ml (2 tsp) oil

5 ml (1 tsp) butter

1–2 cloves garlic, crushed

2 spring onions, chopped

1 small red chilli, seeded and chopped

1 ml (¼ tsp) turmeric

2 ml (½ tsp) ground cumin

250 ml (9 fl oz) thick Bulgarian yoghurt

30 ml (2 tbsp) chopped fresh coriander leaves

a pinch each of salt and sugar

Heat the oil and butter in a small pan, add the garlic, onions and chilli and stir for 1 minute. Add the spices and stir for another minute over low heat. Mix the yoghurt with the coriander and seasoning, add the spice mixture and fold over until smoothly combined. Spoon into a glass jar, cover and refrigerate until needed.

45 ml (3 tbsp) oil

30 ml (2 tbsp) butter

2 medium to large onions,
   sliced into thin rings

3 cloves garlic, crushed

1–2 red peppers, seeded and slivered

30 ml (2 tbsp) curry powder

10 ml (2 tsp) cumin seeds

5 ml (1 tsp) turmeric

250 ml (200 g/7 oz) brown rice

200 ml (160 g/5½ oz) brown
   lentils, picked over and rinsed

1.125 litres (2 pints) hot vegetable
   stock

2 sticks cinnamon

3 bay leaves

60 ml (4 tbsp) currants

a little salt

about 60 g (2 oz) toasted almond
   slivers OR half almonds, half
   sunflower seeds

a handful of chopped parsley

1 x 4-egg omelette, slivered

Heat the oil and butter in a heavy, wide-based saucepan – use a large pan as the ingredients need to be spread over the base. Add the onions and sauté until golden, then add the garlic, peppers, curry powder, cumin and turmeric and toss over low heat for 1 minute. Add the rice and lentils, toss until well mixed, slowly stir in the stock, then add the remaining ingredients, except the almonds, parsley and omelette. Using a fork, place most of the onion rings on top of the mixture, then cover and simmer very gently – you should not hear it popping or spitting – for about 1 hour. At the end of the cooking time the stock should be absorbed, but the mixture still nicely moist. Cover with a cloth and then the lid, and leave to steam for about 10 minutes (make the omelette in this time). Discard the cinnamon and bay leaves, fork in the almonds and parsley, tip onto a large heated platter and top with the omelette.

SERVES 6.

Saucy Beans with Lentils and Butternut

If you're looking for a splendidly nourishing, no-fuss dish, try this bright mixture of **red lentils** and **borlotti beans** in a **chunky sauce**. The creamy-textured Italian beans are readily available in cans and make a super change from the beans we normally use. Splendid served on a bed of **brown rice**, or as a topping for baked **potatoes**.

30 ml (2 tbsp) oil

1 large onion, chopped

2–3 cloves garlic, crushed

7 ml (1½ tsp) each ground
    cumin and coriander

2 ml (½ tsp) each ground
    cinnamon and ginger

400 g (14 oz) butternut, peeled
    and diced (prepared weight)

500 ml (18 fl oz) hot vegetable stock

200 ml (7 fl oz) tomato purée
    (see p. 208)

75 ml (5 tbsp) red lentils, rinsed

a little salt and sugar

1 x 400 g (14 oz) can borlotti
    beans, drained and rinsed

chopped parsley or coriander
    leaves, or both

Heat the oil in a large, deep saucepan, add the onion and garlic and, when softened, reduce the heat, mix in the spices, sizzle briefly, then add the butternut and toss until coated. Add the stock, tomato purée, lentils and seasoning to taste (the amount of salt needed depends, as always, on the saltiness of the stock). Cover and simmer very gently, stirring now and then, for about 20 minutes or until the butternut is soft. Add the beans and simmer for 5 minutes – if necessary, add a little more stock to keep the mixture succulent. Swirl in the parsley and/or coriander and check seasoning – you might wish to add a bite with a few drops of Tabasco.

SERVES 4–6.

Nutty Mushroom and Sprout Stir-fry with Rice and Lentils

Chock-full of nourishing things, this is an absolutely thumping dish for hungry vegetarians and it's ultra-quick to make if you have the **rice** and **lentils** ready cooked. Serve topped with poached **eggs**.

45 ml (3 tbsp) oil

2 medium onions, sliced into thin rings

1 large red pepper, cored and slivered

2–3 cloves garlic, crushed

125 g (4½ oz) white or brown mushrooms, wiped and sliced

45 ml (3 tbsp) soy sauce

45 ml (3 tbsp) sherry

4 x 250 ml (about 550 g/1¼ lb) combined, cooked rice and lentils*

1 x 410 g (14 oz) can bean sprouts, rinsed and drained

125 ml (4½ fl oz) vegetable stock

a handful of chopped parsley

125 ml (60 g/2 oz) roasted sunflower seeds, cashew nuts or slivered almonds

a little butter

4–6 poached eggs

Use a very large pan as the ingredients are bulky (a 28 cm/ 11 in diameter should be just right). Heat the oil, add the onions, pepper, garlic and mushrooms and sauté, tossing constantly, until the onion rings are golden and the mushrooms begin to shrivel. Reduce heat, stir in the soy sauce and sherry and, when bubbling, add the remaining ingredients, except the butter and eggs. Cover and simmer gently to combine the flavours and, when very hot, fork in the butter to moisten, and a little extra soy sauce to flavour if necessary. Top each serving with a softly poached egg.

SERVES 4–6.

* The exact weight will vary as the cooked brown rice and lentils can be used in any ratio, but the total quantity should equal four large cupfuls.

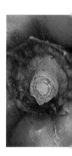

Crunchy Bulgur, Chickpea and Vegetable Salad

250 ml (180 g/6½ oz) bulgur

DRESSING
100 ml (3½ fl oz) oil
45 ml (3 tbsp) lemon juice
15 ml (1 tbsp) honey
5 ml (1 tsp) ground cumin
2 ml (½ tsp) ground coriander
1 small clove garlic, crushed

SALAD
1 x 400 g (14 oz) can chickpeas,
    drained
500 ml (60 g/2 oz) shredded spinach
1 medium red pepper, seeded, diced
a handful of chopped parsley
a few spring onions, chopped
1 large stick table celery, plus
    leaves, chopped
75 ml (5 tbsp) toasted sunflower
    seeds
45 ml (3 tbsp) currants
salt to taste
2 medium tomatoes, diced
fresh coriander leaves and toasted
    sesame seeds to garnish

Place the bulgur in a bowl, add cold water to cover generously and stand for 45 minutes. Make the dressing by combining all the ingredients and set to one side. Drain the bulgur in a fine sieve and squeeze out all the water with your hands, then tip it into a large bowl. Fork in the dressing and, when well mixed, add the remaining ingredients, except the tomatoes. Combine well, using a fork to break up any clumps of bulgur. Cover loosely and stand for 1–2 hours for the flavours to develop. Just before serving, fork in the tomatoes, check seasoning, then spoon onto a platter and scatter with coriander and sesame seeds. Leftovers can be refrigerated for a day or two, but it is unlikely that there will be any.

SERVES 5–6.

Spicy Chickpea and Vegetable Stew

A delightful dish for a vegetarian bash. It has a slight bite, loads of **flavour**, is beautifully **succulent**, makes a huge amount (which is easily halved for a handful of diners) and can be prepared in advance. Serve with **couscous** or **brown rice**, and a bowl of thick natural **yoghurt**.

60 ml (4 tbsp) oil
2 large onions, sliced into thin rings
20 ml (4 tsp) ground cumin
20 ml (4 tsp) ground coriander
500 g (1 lb 2 oz) brinjals, cubed,
    dégorged, rinsed and patted dry
350 g (12 oz) baby marrows, pared
    and diced (prepared weight)
2 large sticks table celery,
    plus some leaves, sliced
3–4 cloves garlic, crushed
2 x 410 g (14 oz) cans tomatoes,
    chopped, plus juice
30 ml (2 tbsp) honey
2 fat sticks cinnamon
30–45 ml (2–3 tbsp) thick chilli sauce
2 x 400 g (14 oz) cans chickpeas,
    drained
500 ml (18 fl oz) vegetable stock
4 bay leaves
fresh coriander leaves for topping

Heat the oil in a very large saucepan, add the onions and, when softening, mix in the cumin and coriander. Sizzle briefly, then add the brinjals, marrows and celery, toss until well mixed and smelling delicious – if necessary add a dash of water to prevent sticking. Add the remaining ingredients, stir to mix, season lightly, then cover and simmer very gently, stirring a few times, for about 25 minutes or until the vegetables are soft. If working ahead, turn into a suitable container and cool. This stew is nicely moist and succulent, but if re-heated may require a little extra stock. Spoon into a large, heated dish and sprinkle with plenty of coriander (roasted cashew nuts are also great, but this is optional).

SERVES 8–10.

Lentil and Apple Curry

The fact that this dish is both cheap and carefree doesn't mean that it isn't nice. It's delicious, and the combination of protein and fibre makes an excellent vegetarian meal. If you have the **lentils** and some **brown rice** ready-cooked (they can be done at any time during the day), all you need do is make the **sauce** shortly before dinner. You can stretch the number of servings too, by adding more lentils and stock – it's one of those obliging dishes that you can play by ear.

250 ml (200 g/7 oz) brown lentils, picked over and rinsed

30 ml (2 tbsp) oil

1 large onion, chopped

3 cloves garlic, crushed

30 ml (2 tbsp) curry powder

5 ml (1 tsp) each ground cumin and turmeric

1 x 410 g (14 oz) can tomatoes, chopped, plus juice

2 sweet apples, peeled and diced

60 ml (4 tbsp) seedless raisins

1–2 sticks cinnamon

15 ml (1 tbsp) honey

5 ml (1 tsp) salt

250 ml (9 fl oz) vegetable stock or water

3 bay leaves

90 ml (6 tbsp) sunflower seeds

Simmer the lentils in 600 ml (1 pint) lightly salted water in a covered saucepan over a low heat for about 50 minutes – all the liquid should be absorbed, and the lentils holding their shape, don't let them become mushy. Heat the oil in a large frying pan, add the onion and garlic and, when softening, add the curry powder, cumin and turmeric and stir-fry briefly, adding a dash of water if necessary. Add the remaining ingredients, except the lentils and sunflower seeds, cover and simmer for 15 minutes. Add the lentils and seeds, cover and cook gently for a further 10–15 minutes. The mixture should be quite juicy – once it comes off the boil it will thicken up – and it needs to be moist enough to serve on rice. Discard the cinnamon and bay leaves and serve with a green salad and bowls of chutney and yoghurt on the side.

SERVES 4–6.

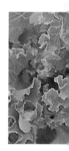

Masala Vegetable and Bean Stew

Many people are miffy about **soya beans**, but they are a very important source of protein in a vegetarian diet. If preferred, however, use another cooked, dried bean, or **chickpeas** – and for a really rib-sticking meal, increase the quantity.

60 ml (4 tbsp) oil
2 medium onions, chopped
2 plump cloves garlic, crushed
10 ml (2 tsp) ground coriander
5 ml (1 tsp) each ground cumin
    and fennel
15–20 ml (3–4 tsp) masala for
    mild curry
300 g (11 oz) firm pumpkin or
    butternut, peeled and cubed
    (prepared weight)
300 g (11 oz) cauliflower or
    broccoli florets
200 g (7 oz) baby marrows, pared
    and sliced (prepared weight)
200 g (7 oz) green beans, sliced
375 ml (13 fl oz) vegetable stock
1 x 410 g (14 oz) can tomatoes,
    chopped, plus juice
salt and a little sugar to taste
2 bay leaves
250 ml (180 g/6½ oz) cooked soya
    beans
60 ml (4 tbsp) fresh coriander leaves

Heat the oil in a very large saucepan – diameter about 28 cm (11 in). Add the onions and garlic and, when softened, add the coriander, cumin, fennel and masala. Stir until sizzling, add the fresh vegetables, toss until well combined, then add the stock and remaining ingredients, except the beans and coriander. Cover and simmer gently for 10 minutes, then give it a stir and continue cooking, covered, over low heat until the vegetables are tender – about 15 minutes more. Add the beans and coriander and, if necessary, a little more stock to ensure a succulent stew. Heat through until piping hot, check seasoning, and serve on a bed of yellow bulgur* with bowls of chutney or mango atjar (for a touch of fire) and thick yoghurt.
SERVES 6–8.

* Fry a few chopped spring onions and some peeled, chopped fresh ginger, with 2 ml (½ tsp) turmeric in a little oil and butter, then add 250 ml (180 g/6½ oz) bulgur, 600 ml (1 pint) hot water, a handful of currants and a pinch of salt. Stir, cover and simmer for about 20 minutes. Fluff up with a fork before serving.

Spiced Lentil and Vegetable Salad with Yoghurt

There are lentil salads and lentil salads and those who have only encountered the mushy, earthy-flavoured versions are in for a pleasant surprise. This one turns out tops for three reasons: the lentils used are the large, green ones which keep their shape when cooked (they are used for sprouting and are available at wholefood

stores); the *raw vegetables* add vitamins and texture; and the *spices* pack in a zesty flavour. Add a topping of thinly segmented *avocado*, surround with wedges of *hard-boiled eggs*, and serve with a bowl of *yoghurt** swirled with *fresh mint* for a whackingly good meal-in-a-salad.

DRESSING

125 ml (4½ fl oz) oil
7 ml (1½ tsp) ground cumin
7 ml (1½ tsp) ground coriander
45 ml (3 tbsp) lemon juice
15 ml (1 tbsp) honey

SALAD

375 ml (270 g/10 oz) large lentils,
  picked over and rinsed
800 ml (1½ pints) water
5 ml (1 tsp) salt
5 ml (1 tsp) turmeric
4 cloves
4–6 spring onions, chopped
500 ml (60 g/2 oz) finely
  shredded spinach
2 large carrots, coarsely grated
125 ml (60 g/2 oz) toasted
  sunflower seeds
a handful of chopped parsley

avocado and hard-boiled eggs
  for the topping

Mix all the ingredients for the dressing, then set aside. Boil the lentils in the water with the salt, turmeric and cloves – keep at a low simmer and do not stir, but check once in case more water is needed. They should be cooked in about 50 minutes. Drain if necessary, tip into a large bowl, remove cloves and immediately fork in the dressing. Add the remaining salad ingredients, tossing well without breaking up the lentils. Cool, then cover loosely and stand for 1–2 hours, then toss again before serving with suggested accompaniments.

SERVES 6.

* For the Yoghurt Dressing, use 250 ml (9 fl oz) Bulgarian yoghurt and 125 ml (4½ fl oz) cultured sour cream marbled with fresh mint or coriander leaves, chives and a drizzle of honey.

Vegetable, Coconut and Cashew Curry

Using a can of *coconut cream* and commercial *red-curry paste* makes this dish a great deal easier than it looks. Nevertheless, preparing a lot of vegetables does take time and so – I blush to admit this – I sometimes start off with a plate of crudités (on offer at certain supermarkets) and then I add a bit of this and that to make up the required quantity. Use vegetables that need approximately the same cooking time. The sauce is creamy and rich with a mild tingle of spices – if you want it hot, add chillies or *chilli powder* to taste. Serve with *Aromatic Rice* (see p. 177).

45 ml (3 tbsp) oil

2 medium onions, chopped

3 cloves garlic, crushed

15 ml (1 tbsp) peeled,
  chopped root ginger

10 ml (2 tsp) ground cumin

45 ml (3 tbsp) red-curry paste

1 kg (2¼ lb) vegetables of
  your choice (prepared weight)*

250 ml (9 fl oz) vegetable stock
  or water

1 x 400 g (14 oz) can coconut
  cream, well shaken

5 ml (1 tsp) finely grated
  lemon rind

5 ml (1 tsp) salt

45 ml (3 tbsp) Thai fish sauce**

15 ml (1 tbsp) soy sauce

5 ml (1 tsp) cornflour

60 ml (4 tbsp) fresh coriander
  leaves

plenty of chopped, roasted cashew
  nuts to garnish

Heat the oil in a very large saucepan – mine has a diameter of 28 cm (11 in). (I don't use a wok here as the vegetables should be spread out to cook evenly.) Add the onions, garlic, ginger, cumin and curry paste and stir for a few minutes to soften the onions. Add all the vegetables, toss until well mixed, then add the stock or water, coconut cream, lemon rind and salt. Cover and simmer for about 20 minutes until cooked, stirring once or twice. Mix the remaining ingredients, except the nuts, stir into the mixture, and allow to bubble and thicken. Top with nuts and serve.

SERVES 6.

* For the vegetables, I use baby marrows, table celery, cauliflower, carrots, broccoli, butternut and red pepper. Once prepared (sliced, julienned, diced or chopped), the weight must be 1 kg (2¼ lb).
** Omit if strictly vegetarian.

Golden Rice with Curried Mushrooms

This bright and **spicy rice** dish can be served hot as an accompaniment, or cold as a salad. Because it looks especially inviting centred at a buffet, the recipe is geared for lots of servings, but the quantities can easily be halved.

500 ml (400 g/14 oz) white
  or brown rice
6 cloves
5 ml (1 tsp) turmeric
2 sticks cinnamon
oil
2 very large onions, sliced into
  thin rings
3 cloves garlic, crushed
30 ml (2 tbsp) curry powder
10 ml (2 tsp) each ground
  cumin and coriander
400 g (14 oz) white mushrooms,
  wiped and thinly sliced
7 ml (1½ tsp) salt
60 ml (4 tbsp) lemon juice
60 ml (4 tbsp) chopped parsley
60 ml (4 tbsp) chopped fresh
  coriander leaves
roasted cashew nuts or
  almonds to garnish*

Boil the rice in lightly salted water with the cloves, turmeric and cinnamon. (Brown rice will require more water and a longer cooking period than white rice – do what you usually do, or follow the instructions on the packet.) Meanwhile, heat the oil in a very large frying pan. If the dish is to be served as a salad, use 125 ml (4½ fl oz); if it is to be an accompaniment, use 60 ml (4 tbsp). Keeping the heat low, sauté the onions and garlic, then add the spices and sizzle briefly before adding the mushrooms and salt. Toss until the mushrooms are yellow and just beginning to shrink, then add the lemon juice and remove from heat. Tip the cooked rice (which must be dry and fluffy) into a large, heated serving dish, or a salad bowl, discard the cinnamon and cloves, and fork in the mushroom mixture together with the parsley and coriander. Sprinkle with nuts and serve immediately, or cool and serve at room temperature.
SERVES 12.

* Sunflower seeds may be substituted if preferred – fork in a handful when you add the herbs.

Aromatic Rice

Everyone suddenly runs out of certain ingredients at times, but it's funny how there are some out of which one runs more suddenly than others. With my neighbour, it's Worcestershire sauce. With me, it's Basmati. Now I see it, now I don't. And it's usually when I'm on the verge of making a curry that I don't. That's when I turn to this alternative. It works like a dream and has this bonus: you simply bring it to the boil, then turn off the heat and leave it alone – for hours, if you like. At dinner time, add a little water and reheat gently.

30 ml (2 tbsp) oil

1 medium onion, finely chopped

7 ml (1½ tsp) cumin seeds

15 ml (1 tbsp) mustard seeds

5 ml (1 tsp) turmeric

4 cardamom pods, bruised

4 cloves

375 ml (300 g/11 oz) long-grain
   white rice, rinsed and drained

900 ml (1½ pints) water

3 bay leaves

5 ml (1 tsp) salt

Heat the oil and gently fry the onion and spices for about one minute – keep the heat low as the seeds tend to burn easily. Add the rice and toss until coated. Add the remaining ingredients, bring to the boil, then switch off the stove plate, cover and leave if working ahead, otherwise simmer until done. Remove the cardamom, cloves and bay leaves before serving.

SERVES 6.

Couscous Salad with Spicy Sautéed Vegetables

Make plenty, because this colourful mix of fabulous flavours is quite the nicest of **couscous salads.** Don't be fazed by the list of ingredients, they're all quite basic, and the salad is really easy to make.

60 ml (4 tbsp) oil

10 ml (2 tsp) each ground
coriander and cumin

5 ml (1 tsp) peeled, chopped
root ginger

2 ml (½ tsp) ground cinnamon

1 brinjal (200 g/7 oz), sliced
into small chunks, dégorged,
rinsed and patted dry

1 large red pepper, seeded and diced

2 cloves garlic, crushed

250 ml (170 g/6 oz) quick-
cooking couscous

turmeric

60 ml (4 tbsp) sunflower seeds

60 ml (4 tbsp) currants

60 ml (4 tbsp) fresh coriander leaves

4–6 spring onions, chopped

45 ml (3 tbsp) olive oil

10 ml (2 tsp) lemon juice

10 ml (2 tsp) honey

fresh coriander to garnish

Heat the oil in a large frying pan, reduce heat to low, add the spices and toss for 30 seconds. Add the brinjal, pepper and garlic, toss to coat with the spices, then cover and simmer very gently until cooked, tossing occasionally. You should not have to add any liquid, as juices will form if heat is kept very low, but add a sprinkling of water if necessary. The vegetables should be cooked in 8–10 minutes. Meanwhile prepare the couscous – follow the packet instructions, adding a little turmeric: I use 2 ml (½ tsp) to 375 ml (13 fl oz) salted boiling water. Remove the frying pan from the stove and gently fork in the fluffed-up couscous, sunflower seeds, currants, coriander and onions. Mix the oil, lemon juice and honey and fork into the mixture – work quickly and lightly to prevent the couscous from clumping. Check seasoning and turn into a large salad bowl. Allow to cool, then cover loosely and set aside for about 2 hours, or refrigerate. Garnish and serve.
SERVES 6–8.

Nutty Brown Rice and Mushroom Salad

I have a friend (friend?) who regularly calls to say: 'You are invited to lunch on condition that you bring a big bowl of your rice and mushroom salad.'

250 ml (200 g/7 oz) brown rice

600 ml (1 pint) water

75 ml (5 tbsp) oil

200 g (7 oz) brown mushrooms,
  wiped and sliced

2 cloves garlic, crushed

1 large red pepper, seeded
  and diced

1 sprig fresh rosemary

6 spring onions, chopped

a handful of chopped parsley

30 ml (2 tbsp) lemon juice

30 ml (2 tbsp) soy sauce

a pinch of sugar

250 ml (60 g/2 oz) lentil sprouts

1 large carrot, coarsely grated

60 ml (4 tbsp) sunflower seeds

To cook the rice, oil the base of a heavy saucepan, add the rice, water and a little salt, bring to the boil, then cover and simmer over very low heat for about 50 minutes. Meanwhile, heat the oil in a large frying pan, add the mushrooms, garlic, red pepper and rosemary and stir-fry until the mushrooms start to brown. Remove the pan from the stove, add the onions, parsley, lemon juice, soy sauce and sugar and set aside, covered, until the rice is cooked. Tip the hot rice into a salad bowl and immediately fork in the mushroom mixture, adding all the juices from the pan, but discarding the rosemary. Toss in the sprouts, carrot and sunflower seeds, cool, then cover loosely until ready to serve. SERVES 6.

179

* Rice – whether white or brown – usually needs to be rinsed before cooking. Drain well.

desserts

Given the disasters I've had with desserts, I sometimes wonder why I continue to make them. Once, just before serving lunch, a bird flew through the pantry window and sat on my **trifle**. Another time, a gecko fell from the diningroom ceiling and disappeared into the chocolate **mousse**. Then there was the day a guest found my labrador's licence disc in his serving of Christmas **pudding**. But I press on because I enjoy desserts, they round off a dinner neatly, and guests seem to feel cheated without one. They can, however, make a hostess nervous. My friends tell me they make desserts only when entertaining, or for important gatherings, and for this reason preparing the final course has ceased to be fun. It has become a huge, fat challenge.

It was easier in the old days. Judging from the mothy old books on Household Management in my kitchen library, desserts (usually listed in the indexes after Dentures and before Dewlaps and Dizziness) were normally quite simple affairs: stewed prunes or jelly or junket, maybe Chocolate Castles or Apple Hedgehog or Gooseberry Grunt on smarter occasions. But times have changed, and these days one is prepared to go to a great deal of trouble and expense, as long as the final result has people making happy little noises while eating them. Like **Mmmm** and Hmmm and Ummm ... any hostess will recognize the tune and no Gooseberry Grunt or Stewed Prune will ever strike the right note.

It seems it has to be something full of eggs and sugar and chocolate and **cream**. And yet many people today are either on a diet, or should be on a diet, so I believe one shouldn't go completely over the top. I've been at a dinner where a guest had one taste, blanched, put down her spoon and said Darling, It's Absolutely Delicious, Quite Quite Lovely, But I Can't, I Positively Cannot. (It was a mousse – you know the kind – 12 egg yolks, a litre of cream, a brick of butter and four chocolate bars, that one.) And so I have included a **fruity** offering or two in this chapter, and have slightly scaled down the quantities of rich stuff in some of the other recipes, but nevertheless not one of these desserts is either fat-free, sugar-free or kilojoule-free, and some more so than others, if you get my meaning. That said, the decision to indulge now rests solely on your shoulders. And probably elsewhere too, in the end.

PS There is an extraordinary cold fruity pud which you can make by simmering 500 g (1 lb 2 oz) cooking apples, peeled and sliced, with 200 ml (7 fl oz) apple juice, 60 ml (4 tbsp) water, 2 ml (½ tsp) each ground cinnamon and vanilla essence, 90 g (3¼ oz) chopped, pitted dates and 30 g (1 oz) chopped pecan nuts for about 12 minutes, covered, stirring now and then until soft – add a spoon of honey if you wish. It looks awful but it's sweet and naturally wholesome.

desserts

Honeyed Strawberries Romanoff

I find it impossible to ignore a punnet of ripe **red strawberries**. They're wicked little things, the way they wink and beckon at you, and I fall for them every time. What about a pavlova then? Or a brilliant mousse? A pink ice cream? Often these would take the time I haven't got – and that's when this dessert helps me out. It's definitely different from plain sugared berries, but almost as quick to prepare and, unlike the classic **Romanoff** with cubed sugar and Curaçao, this version requires ingredients you are sure to have on hand. This is a good choice when you want an easy but elegant dessert to end a smart dinner – it's not too sweet, it's delicately flavoured with **orange**, and perfect with **ice cream** or Chantilly **cream**.

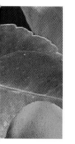

600 g (1¼ lb) ripe, red strawberries
125 ml (4½ fl oz) fresh orange juice
45 ml (3 tbsp) runny honey
60 ml (4 tbsp) Van der Hum liqueur
2 ml (½ tsp) very finely grated
    orange rind

Rinse, hull, pat dry, and then halve or quarter strawberries. Spoon into a fairly wide, shallow dish – a 20 cm (8 in) pie dish is just right. Mix the remaining ingredients, pour over the strawberries, toss to mix, then cover with cling wrap and refrigerate for at least 6 hours, but better still overnight.
SERVES 6.

Cream Cheese Ices with Strawberry Coulis

Rather like crustless little cheesecakes, individually moulded and frozen, turned out and nestled on a pool of bright, puréed berries – this dessert could hardly be prettier, and it takes only minutes to make. The mixture may be frozen in any large ice cream container, but for stylish presentation you will need freezerproof ramekins – use small ones, as it's a rich dessert.

500 g (1 lb/2 oz) cream cheese OR
   250 g (9 oz) each cream cheese
   and smooth, low-fat cottage
   cheese (see p. 208)
250 ml (200 g/7 oz) caster sugar
3 extra-large eggs, separated
10 ml (2 tsp) vanilla essence
250 ml (9 fl oz) cream, whipped
sprigs of fresh mint, plain or
   frosted, to decorate

STRAWBERRY COULIS
250 g (9 oz) strawberries, hulled,
   rinsed and sliced
30 ml (2 tbsp) caster sugar

Whisk cheese, sugar, egg yolks and vanilla until smooth. Fold in cream and egg whites stiffly whisked with a pinch of salt. Combine gently but thoroughly. Place a large circle of cling wrap in each of 10 ramekins, leaving sufficient overlap to allow you to lift the ices right out when frozen. Spoon mixture into each, filling to the top, and freeze for about 4 hours, until firm. Make the coulis by placing ingredients in a blender. Leave for a short while to draw juices, then blend until smooth. Unmould cheese creams onto individual serving plates and surround with a drizzle of coulis.

SERVES 10.

Evergreen
Chocolate Mousse

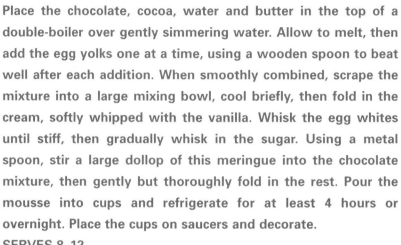

200 g (7 oz) dark chocolate,
  broken into chunks
10 ml (2 tsp) cocoa powder
30 ml (2 tbsp) water
10 ml (2 tsp) butter
4 extra large eggs, separated
250 ml (9 fl oz) cream
a few drops of vanilla essence
30 ml (2 tbsp) caster sugar

Place the chocolate, cocoa, water and butter in the top of a double-boiler over gently simmering water. Allow to melt, then add the egg yolks one at a time, using a wooden spoon to beat well after each addition. When smoothly combined, scrape the mixture into a large mixing bowl, cool briefly, then fold in the cream, softly whipped with the vanilla. Whisk the egg whites until stiff, then gradually whisk in the sugar. Using a metal spoon, stir a large dollop of this meringue into the chocolate mixture, then gently but thoroughly fold in the rest. Pour the mousse into cups and refrigerate for at least 4 hours or overnight. Place the cups on saucers and decorate.
SERVES 8–12.

CHOCOLATE DIPPED STRAWBERRIES
These look good on anything short of a curry, and are stunning on a chocolate mousse. Use ripe, firm berries complete with calyx and a length of stem. Rinse and dry very well. For the dip, I use dark *cooking* chocolate. Break it into chunks and melt with the merest dash of water in a small container. Holding the berries by the stems, dip the pointed ends into the melted chocolate, swirling to coat, then place on a sheet of greaseproof paper to set. Use within a couple of hours.

* For a mocha-flavoured mousse, add 10 ml (2 tsp) pure, instant coffee powder and 30 ml (2 tbsp) coffee liqueur when melting the chocolate with the cocoa, water and butter.

Spiced Oranges with Citrus-tea Sorbet

This is a seriously stylish dessert: refreshing, interesting, and about as different from apple pie as you can get. The tangy **sorbet**, with its surprising hint of **tea**, offsets the sweetness of the macerated **oranges**, and if ever you need to woo jaded palates, this is surely the way to go. The ice cream is a very rich alternative to the sorbet. Whichever one you choose, place a scoop (or a single quenelle, shaped with two spoons) in the centre of the plate, surround with the oranges and drizzle with a little of the **syrup**.

125 ml (100 g/3½ oz) granulated sugar
250 ml (9 fl oz) water
1 fat stick cinnamon, halved
6 cloves
1 walnut-sized knob root ginger, peeled and chopped
3 x 5 cm (2 in) strips orange peel (no pith)
5 large sweet oranges

Place all the ingredients, except the oranges, in a saucepan, stir over low heat until the sugar has dissolved, then increase the heat and boil without stirring for 5 minutes. Cool. Meanwhile peel the oranges – make sure you remove all the white pith. Slice the oranges into thin rounds, flicking out any pips as you go, and place in a large, shallow bowl – a 23 cm (9 in) pie dish is ideal. Pour over any juices from the cutting board, then strain over the cooled syrup. Cover and refrigerate for up to 24 hours. SERVES 6.

Sorbet

Sorbets really need either to be churned in an ice cream machine, or frozen and beaten and frozen and beaten several times to achieve a good texture. Adding gelatine is cheating a bit, but it does simplify the process and helps to smooth it out.

600 ml (1 pint) water
100 ml (85 g/3 oz) caster sugar
5 ml (1 tsp) finely grated
   orange rind
10 ml (2 tsp) gelatine
60 ml (4 tbsp) lemon juice
60 ml (4 tbsp) orange juice
45 ml (3 tbsp) honey
3 tea bags

In a small, deep saucepan bring the water, sugar and orange rind to a slow boil, stirring to dissolve the sugar, then increase the heat and boil rapidly for 5 minutes. Meanwhile sponge the gelatine in the mixed lemon and orange juice. Remove the hot syrup from the heat, stir in the gelatine and honey and add the tea bags. Stand for 15 minutes, remove the tea bags, then pour the mixture into a jug. Leave to cool, then strain into a shallow freezer container and freeze for about 1½ hours until as firm as a soft jelly. Turn into a processor fitted with the metal blade and whizz until smoothly liquefied. Pour the mixture back into its container and freeze until solid. If made more than 4 hours in advance, transfer to the refrigerator until it is soft enough to scoop.

Orange Ice Cream

The honey and brandy prevent this ice cream from setting hard, and it can be served straight from the freezer – one small scoop per serving.

2 extra large eggs, separated
45 ml (3 tbsp) caster sugar
30 ml (2 tbsp) honey
15 ml (1 tbsp) finely grated
   orange rind
30 ml (2 tbsp) brandy
250 ml (9 fl oz) cream, softly whipped
lemon juice
2 ml (½ tsp) vanilla essence

Whisk the egg yolks, sugar, honey, orange rind and brandy very well until the mixture is light and butter-coloured. Fold in the cream, egg whites (which have been stiffly whisked with a few drops of lemon juice), and vanilla. Fold over until smoothly combined, pour into a 2 litre (3½ pints) freezer container and freeze.

Coconut Ice Cream with Lavender and Litchis

The title lies: there is no lavender whatsoever in this **ice cream**, but the thought of something tasting of lavender is so enticing that I've slipped it in. Trouble is, I have never been able to capture that rare fragrance in a dish, but a decorative sprig of this beautiful **herb** certainly looks good enough to eat. Place a scoop of the sweet ice cream in each small bowl, surround with slivered **litchis** (fresh is best – if canned, add a little of the syrup as well) and top with a sprig of **lavender**.

500 ml (18 fl oz) milk
250 ml (9 fl oz) cream
300 ml (95 g/3¼ oz) desiccated
   coconut
2 extra large eggs
1 extra large egg yolk
45 ml (3 tbsp) honey
   (must be light and thin)
100 ml (85 g/3 oz) caster sugar
a pinch of salt
7 ml (1½ tsp) cornflour
2 ml (½ tsp) vanilla essence
litchis

Mix the milk, cream and coconut and bring just to boiling point over very low heat. Set aside for about 30 minutes to let the flavours infuse. In a large mixing bowl, whisk together the eggs, the extra yolk, honey, sugar, salt and cornflour. Pour the coconut cream through a fine mesh sieve into the egg mixture and use a wooden spoon to extract all the liquid. Reserve 30 ml (2 tbsp) of the coconut left in the sieve and discard the rest. Pour the custard mixture into the top of a double boiler and stir over simmering water until it thickens. Stir in the reserved coconut and vanilla and when cool pour into a freezer container and freeze until it starts to firm up. Return to the mixing bowl and beat well, then freeze until solid. If you have made the ice cream well in advance, transfer from the freezer to the refrigerator about 30 minutes before serving, to soften a little.
MAKES 6 LARGE SCOOPS.

A **fruit-topped cheesecake** always reminds me of a pub in a small village in Yorkshire. I spent a week at a B&B in this village, and every night I fell into this pub, after walking the moors. This is a very peaceful and cold thing to do. Purple heather; muddy puddles; lonely farmhouses; prattling streams; sloshy bogs; baleful sheep. The wind was icy, the rain was wet, it was lovely. And I soon found that a visit to the pub at the end of the day made it even lovelier.

It wasn't just the cider – although the sight of that bubbly amber liquid wooshing out at the pull of a lever did warm my cockles. And it certainly wasn't the pies, or the baked potatoes, and definitely not the sweetcorn and tuna. It was the *cheesecake*. This pub had a long, polished bar counter beneath which was a glass display case, and here the cheesecakes sat smiling beneath their brilliant, gelatinous toppings of *fruit*. Now, when you're far from home and your purse is thin and your tooth is sweet, happiness lies in ending the day with a slice of cheesecake. A slice of cheesecake, with *cream*. There was a nice local lad in charge of these cakes, and after slicing and serving them, he would wander between the tables waving a can of cream like a fire extinguisher (you know the cream – it's the kind that squirts out under pressure). All you had to do was put up your hand and you'd get a free wriggle on your plate. When you're a tourist on a budget you'll take anything that's free. He soon recognised this and, being a nice guy, took to flourishing his fire extinguisher without my even having to ask. Sometimes he simply sprayed fat white ribbons all over my slice. At other times he'd make intricate patterns, and then stand back, head tilted sideways, admiring his artwork. But when he was busy he would just aim and squirt in passing. Sometimes he hit the cloth. Once he got my head. But I loved the whole ritual. I even liked the canned cream.

Cheesecake with Fruit Topping

This is a very large, snow-white **cheesecake** topped with **glazed pears** or bright **cherries**, and spiked with a splosh of **liqueur**.

Line base and sides of a greased 23 cm x 6 cm (9 in x 2¼ in) pie dish with a biscuit crust and refrigerate.

FILLING
25 ml (5 tsp) gelatine
75 ml (5 tbsp) water
3 extra large egg whites
200 ml (170 g/6 oz) caster sugar
250 g (9 oz) smooth, low-fat
   cottage cheese (see p. 208)
250 g (9 oz) cream cheese
60 ml (4 tbsp) Amaretto liqueur
   (optional)
250 ml (9 fl oz) cream
5 ml (1 tsp) vanilla essence

TOPPING
1 x 410 g (14 oz) can pears or
   1 x 425 g (15 oz) can stoneless
   black cherries
cornflour

whipped cream and toasted
   almond flakes to decorate

Sponge the gelatine in the water, dissolve over simmering water, then cool slightly before using. Whisk the egg whites. Gradually whisk in half the sugar, whisk to a thick meringue, then set aside. Without washing the beaters, whisk together the cheeses, remaining sugar and liqueur if using. When smooth, add the cream and vanilla and whip until thick. While beating, slowly drizzle in the dissolved gelatine. Fold in the meringue mixture, pour onto the crust and refrigerate until firm.

PEAR TOPPING
Drain pears, reserving juice, pat dry, slice into thin segments and arrange in circles on top of the cheesecake. Slake 5 ml (1 tsp) cornflour with 100 ml (3½ fl oz) pear juice, bring to the boil, stirring, and boil until clear. Cool slightly, then use a pastry brush to paint the pears with the glaze. Refrigerate and decorate before serving.

CHERRY TOPPING
Drain cherries, reserving juice, then chop finely. Mix 150 ml (5¼ fl oz) juice with 15 ml (1 tbsp) cornflour, stir over low heat until bubbling and thick, add the cherries, cool to room temperature, then spread over chilled cheesecake and return to the refrigerator to set.

SERVES 10.

Chocolate Hazelnut Cheesecake

I once had a week-end party for 24 people. This was not as difficult as it sounds, as I was living on a farm at the time – the house was one of those large sprawling homesteads with plenty of bedrooms, and catering was easy with all those cows and hens on tap. Everything went swimmingly until it came to Sunday breakfast. I served scrambled eggs – and one of the guests broke a tooth. Broke a tooth on a scrambled egg? To this day I don't know what it actually hit on, but it, well, came out in bits. Now how would you feel if this happened to you? Especially if you were freshly married? Frankly, I've never got over it – and possibly that is why I tend to avoid anything that could be a crunchy surprise in something that should be soft and smooth. So the *nuts* in this cheesecake are on the bottom and on the top, not in the middle. It's a packed-with-kilojoules cheesecake, but not overly sweet and cloying, and it will feed a crowd.

With regard to *biscuit crusts*: I usually line only the base and not the sides of the dish. Not only does this mean you will need fewer sweet crumbs and less butter, but I think the extra crumby mixture overpowers the delicate flavour of most creamy fillings. For greasing, I use a mixture of oil and butter – about $\frac{1}{3}$ oil to $\frac{2}{3}$ butter – this makes for easier removal.

CRUST

Line the base of a greased 23 cm (9 in) pie dish, 6–7 cm (2¼–2¾ in) deep, with a mixture of 250 ml (90 g/3¼ oz) biscuit crumbs, 125 ml (50 g/1¾ oz) crushed roasted hazelnuts, 10 ml (2 tsp) cocoa powder and just enough melted butter to bind. Press in firmly, then refrigerate while making the filling – have all the ingredients ready because once the gelatine has been added the mixture firms up quickly.

FILLING

250 g (9 oz) smooth, low-fat
  cottage cheese (see p. 208)
250 g (9 oz) cream cheese
90 ml (6 tbsp) caster sugar
3 extra large eggs, separated
15 ml (1 tbsp) cocoa powder
  dissolved in 30 ml (2 tbsp)
  boiling water
200 g (7 oz) dark chocolate,
  broken into chunks
45 ml (3 tbsp) water
25 ml (5 tsp) gelatine
60 ml (4 tbsp) water
250 ml (9 fl oz) cream softly whipped
  with 10 ml (2 tsp) vanilla essence
extra 90 ml (6 tbsp) caster sugar
coarsely crushed hazelnuts for
  topping

Using an electric whisk, beat the cheeses, sugar and egg yolks until smooth, then whisk in the dissolved cocoa. Melt the chocolate in a container with the 45 ml (3 tbsp) water over simmering water, then stir quickly until shiny and smooth. Drop dollops of chocolate into the cheese mixture, whisking well. Sponge the gelatine in the 60 ml (4 tbsp) water, dissolve over hot water and slowly beat into the cheese mixture. (If it is not over-heated, and you drizzle it in slowly while whisking, it should not make 'strings'.) Fold in the vanilla/cream mixture. Whisk the egg whites until stiff, gradually whisk in the extra sugar until it achieves meringue consistency, stir a spoonful into the chocolate mixture, then gently fold in the remainder. Pour the mixture onto the crust, sprinkle with nuts and refrigerate for several hours or overnight.

SERVES 10–12.

Baked Apples and Gooseberries with Rosemary Crumble

In the past **herbs** were usually reserved for savoury dishes, but these days they are creeping in everywhere and putting herbs into a dessert has become a fun thing to do. Here, Granny's **Apple Crumble** is updated by spiking the topping with fresh **rosemary** – it's subtle, but definitely there. Serve with **cream**, floppily whipped with a little icing sugar and a tot of **brandy**.

CRUMBLE

250 ml (120 g/4 oz) cake flour
  (see p. 208)
125 ml (65 g/2 oz) whole-wheat flour
200 ml (160 g/5½ oz) granulated
  sugar
2 ml (½ tsp) grated nutmeg
15 ml (1 tbsp) finely chopped
  fresh rosemary leaves
125 g (4½ oz) cold butter, diced
125 ml (45 g/1½ oz) chopped
  walnuts or pecans

a sprig of flowering rosemary to
  decorate, otherwise leave plain

FILLING

1 x 765 g (1¾ lb) can pie apples, roughly chopped
1 x 410 g (14 oz) can gooseberries, drained
45 ml (3 tbsp) caster sugar
30 ml (2 tbsp) golden syrup
2 ml (½ tsp) ground cinnamon

Mix the fruit, sugar and syrup and spoon into a buttered 23 cm (9 in) pie dish, at least 5 cm/2 in deep to take the thick layer of topping. Sprinkle with cinnamon. Mix both flours, the sugar, nutmeg and rosemary, rub in the butter until crumbly, mix in the nuts, and sprinkle over the top of the fruit. Bake at 180 °C (350 °F, Gas Mark 4) for 45–50 minutes until lightly browned. Serve warm, rather than hot – or bake ahead, and reheat at 160 °C (325 °F, Gas Mark 3).
SERVES 8.

Cinnamon Poached Pears with Nut Liqueur

Luscious **pears** bathed in a liqueur-flavoured **syrup**, with a complementary topping of crushed **nuts** – this is a superb dessert for which you can use either Amaretto and **almonds**, or Frangelico and **hazelnuts**. You can serve the pears plain to relish the fine flavours; with crème fraîche to offset the sweetness; or with a blob of mascarpone piled into the hollows. Elegant, easy, and do-ahead.

4 large pears (700–800 g/1½–1¾ lb), unblemished and not-quite-ripe
lemon juice
500 ml (18 fl oz) water
125 ml (100 g/3½ oz) granulated sugar
2 fat sticks cinnamon
45–60 ml (3–4 tbsp) Amaretto or Frangelico liqueur
toasted almonds or roasted hazelnuts, coarsely crushed, for topping*

* If using hazelnuts, remove loose skins after roasting by rubbing the nuts in a clean kitchen towel.

Peel the pears as smoothly as possible, halve, and nick out the pips and core. Brush the rounded sides with lemon juice. Bring the water, sugar and cinnamon to the boil in a wide-based frying pan. Add the pears, rounded sides up, in a single layer. Cover and simmer gently for about 30 minutes. Test with the tip of a skewer – they should be soft but definitely not mushy. Using a slotted spoon, remove the pears from the poaching liquid and arrange them in a shallow dish to fit snugly, rounded sides up. Discard the cinnamon. Turn up the heat and boil the poaching liquid rapidly, uncovered, for 10–12 minutes, or until very bubbly, a pale toffee in colour, and reduced to about 150 ml (5¼ fl oz). Remove from the stove, stir in the chosen liqueur, and slowly pour the syrup over the pears. Leave to cool, basting a few times, then cover and refrigerate. Sprinkle with nuts before serving. SERVES 4–8.

Light Orange Fluffs

These fluffs belong to the **cheesecake** family, but they have a lower fat content than usual – no crust, egg yolks or full cream. **Evaporated milk** is used instead of the latter – it adds both lightness and volume, and you can't taste it in here. This is altogether a surprisingly good alternative to cheesecake, and easy too – you simply whip, pour and chill.

250 g (9 oz) smooth, low-fat
   cottage cheese (see p. 208)
125 ml (100 g/3½ oz) caster sugar
5 ml (1 tsp) very finely grated
   orange rind
5 ml (1 tsp) vanilla essence
10 ml (2 tsp) gelatine
125 ml (4½ fl oz) fresh orange juice
1 x 165 g (6 oz) can evaporated
   milk, chilled overnight
lemon juice
2 extra large egg whites
a pinch of salt

Use an electric whisk, and have everything ready as preparation needs to be quick. Whisk the cottage cheese, four-fifths of the sugar, the orange rind and vanilla until smooth. Sponge the gelatine in the orange juice, dissolve over simmering water, and slowly drizzle into the cheese mixture, while whisking. Using a chilled bowl, whisk the evaporated milk with a few drops of lemon juice until it has trebled in volume. Fold it into the cheese mixture. Whisk the egg whites with the salt until stiff, then gradually whisk in the remaining sugar. Fold into the cheese mixture, using a metal spoon and, when smoothly combined, pour into glasses and set in the refrigerator.
SERVES 8.

Tropical Fruit Flop

Fruit blanketed with a flop of **cream**, **yoghurt** and melting brown **sugar** has become one of the desserts of the moment, served at many a dinner party, and it's always popular. This version is a favourite as it requires only two fruits, making it a year-round affair – mangoes in summer, papinos in winter. Neither turns brown or mushy on standing, and the litchis come from a can. Complement these fruits with a touch of **ginger**, **Amaretto** and **almonds**, and you can be sure of serving a flop-proof flop.

2 large, ripe, firm mangoes, peeled and cubed (500 g/1 lb 2 oz prepared weight) OR

400 g (14 oz) ripe but firm papinos, peeled, seeded and diced (prepared weight)

1 x 565 g (1 lb 4 oz) can pitted litchis, drained, patted dry and slivered

1 large knob preserved ginger, finely chopped

175 ml (6¼ fl oz) plain, thick Bulgarian yoghurt

30–45 ml (2–3 tbsp) Amaretto liqueur

a few drops of vanilla essence

200 ml (7 fl oz) cream, very stiffly whipped

45 ml (3 tbsp) soft brown sugar

toasted almond flakes to decorate

Mix the prepared fruits and ginger, and spoon into one glass bowl or divide between six small bowls or goblets. Fold the yoghurt, liqueur and vanilla into the cream – the mixture should be thick and spreadable rather than pourable. Cover the fruit completely. Sprinkle with sugar – this quantity is quite enough as the fruit is sweet, the cream is sweet and the Amaretto is sweet – if using individual bowls, simply divide equally. Refrigerate for about 4 hours, by which time the sugar should be starting to melt. Sprinkle with almonds just before serving. SERVES 6.

* Be sure to use fibreless mangoes and not the stringy ones that leave hairy threads between your teeth and taste of turpentine.

Chocolate-orange Dessert

Liqueur-soaked biscuits and a **fudgy chocolate** topping make a dream of a dessert that falls somewhere between a torte and a tart, a russe and a mousse. A seductive indulgence, and easy to prepare.

200 ml (7 fl oz) fresh orange juice

45 ml (3 tbsp) Van der Hum liqueur

125 g (4½ oz) boudoir biscuits

200 g (7 oz) dark, orange-flavoured chocolate*

125 ml (4½ fl oz) water

30 ml (2 tbsp) butter

45 ml (3 tbsp) caster sugar

10 ml (2 tsp) gelatine

45 ml (3 tbsp) water

250 ml (9 fl oz) cream, softly whipped

5 ml (1 tsp) vanilla essence

2 extra large egg whites, stiffly whisked with a pinch of salt

to decorate: as the dessert is not overly sweet, you could use Chantilly cream (cream, lightly sweetened, flavoured with vanilla and whipped), otherwise simply top with chocolate curls

Mix the juice and liqueur in a large, shallow bowl, turn the biscuits in the mixture until thoroughly moistened, then arrange them on the base of a fairly deep, 23 cm (9 in) pie dish. It is important that the base be completely covered – if necessary, break the biscuits to fit. Slowly drizzle over any leftover liquid. Break up the chocolate and melt together with the 125 ml (4½ fl oz) water, butter and sugar, over simmering water. Pour the mixture into a bowl. Sponge the gelatine in the 45 ml (3 tbsp) water, dissolve over low heat, then stir it into the chocolate mixture. Cool until just thickening – you can hurry this by resting the bowl in a container of cold water. Fold in the cream, vanilla and stiff egg whites. Pour the mixture over the biscuit base, spreading evenly, and refrigerate for a few hours until firm, or overnight. Decorate and serve sliced into wedges.

SERVES 8–10.

* If you can't find this type of chocolate, add a teaspoon of finely grated orange rind when melting plain, dark chocolate. This option is definitely second best and you will need to add a little extra sugar. Orange chocolate has just the right, smooth flavour.

Fruity Orange **and** Pecan Carrot Cake

 Dessert cakes, served with the coffee, make appropriate sweet endings to brunches or informal lunches, and a carrot cake lavished with creamy icing is always a favourite. This is a super version – dark, spicy and simply bursting with fruit and flavour.

3 extra large eggs

250 ml (200 g/7 oz) granulated sugar

10 ml (2 tsp) finely grated
  orange rind

250 ml (9 fl oz) oil

500 ml (240 g/9 oz) cake flour
  (see p. 208)

5 ml (1 tsp) bicarbonate of soda

10 ml (2 tsp) baking powder

10 ml (2 tsp) mixed ground spice

a pinch of salt

3 medium carrots (170 g/6 oz),
  coarsely grated

250 ml (150 g/5½ oz) fruit cake
  mixture

30 ml (2 tbsp) orange marmalade

60 g (2 oz) pecan nuts, chopped

ICING

750 ml (390 g/14 oz) sifted
  icing sugar

1 ml (¼ tsp) grated nutmeg

30 ml (2 tbsp) soft butter

about 90 ml (6 tbsp) smooth
  cottage or cream cheese
  (see p. 208)

a few drops of vanilla essence

pecan halves to decorate

Whisk the eggs, sugar and orange rind until light, then whisk in the oil. Sift the flour, bircarbonate of soda, baking powder, ground spice and salt and beat in lightly until combined. Add the remaining ingredients and mix well to a sticky batter. Pour batter into an oiled 21 x 21 x 5 cm (8¼ x 8¼ x 2 in) square tin, or a 22 x 9 cm (8¾ x 3½ in) tube tin, spreading evenly. Bake at 160 °C (325 °F, Gas Mark 3) for about 1 hour – test with a skewer. Stand for 5 minutes before turning it out onto a rack to cool. To make the icing, sift the icing sugar with the nutmeg, whisk in the butter then, using a wooden spoon, mix in the cheese in small dollops – the exact amount depends on how soft the cheese is. Do not add any liquid and do not use an electric whisk. Mix steadily just until the mixture becomes smooth and creamy, then add the vanilla. Spread the icing over the top and sides of the cake, and stud with nuts.

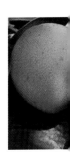

Fruit Salad Calypso with Ginger Cream

Tropical fruits undoubtedly make the best fruit salads, but they are seasonal and not necessarily available at the same time. It may be necessary to use a can or two, as in this favourite recipe which links three fruits with orange and rum. Refreshing on its own, delicious with the flavoured **cream**.

SYRUP
200 ml (7 fl oz) fresh orange juice
30 ml (2 tbsp) lemon juice
60 ml (4 tbsp) granulated sugar
2 sticks cinnamon
8 cloves
5 ml (1 tsp) finely grated
   orange rind
60 ml (4 tbsp) rum

1 ripe pawpaw or papino,
   peeled, seeded and diced
   (700 g/1½ lb prepared weight)
4 large, ripe but firm bananas,
   sliced
2 x 425 g (15 oz) cans mangoes,
   well-drained and chopped

Make the syrup first, as it needs to cool before using. Place all the ingredients, except the rum, in a small saucepan and bring to a slow boil, stirring to dissolve the sugar. Set aside to cool. Place all the prepared fruit in a large glass bowl (it should be wide rather than deep). Stir the rum into the cooled syrup, strain over the fruit, stir gently to mix, then cover and refrigerate for at least 2 hours before serving.
SERVES 8–10.

Whip 250 ml (9 fl oz) cream with 15 ml (1 tbsp) ginger syrup until floppily thick – not stiff. Fold in 30 ml (2 tbsp) finely chopped preserved ginger (to chop, use a pair of kitchen scissors or a sharp knife dipped into hot water). Adding a handful of chopped pecan nuts or walnuts is optional, but delicious. Pile into a bowl and refrigerate.

Kahlúa Chocolate Mousse

I've never been to Kahlúa (has anyone been to Kahlúa?), but I hear they make a lovely local **mousse**, and this is my version, custard-based and dependable.

375 ml (13 fl oz) milk

15 ml (1 tbsp) pure instant coffee granules

15 ml (1 tbsp) cocoa powder

100 g (3½ oz) dark chocolate, roughly chopped

2 extra large eggs, separated

a pinch of salt

45 ml (3 tbsp) caster sugar

10 ml (2 tsp) gelatine

60 ml (4 tbsp) water

60 ml (4 tbsp) Kahlúa or other good coffee liqueur

125 ml (4½ fl oz) cream

2 ml (½ tsp) vanilla essence

to decorate: this is a reasonably modest mousse, so you might want to top it with whipped cream, but it's just as good with a flutter of shaved chocolate

Rinse a heavy-based saucepan with water, then add the milk, coffee, cocoa and chocolate. Slowly bring to just below boiling point, stirring, until the chocolate has melted. Whisk the egg yolks with the salt and half the sugar, pour the hot chocolate-milk into the egg mixture, stir to mix, then return to the saucepan and stir over low heat until the mixture thickens – it must NOT boil, but thicken it must. Remove from the stove and give it a quick whisk. Sprinkle gelatine onto the water, sponge for a minute, then stir it into the hot mixture. When dissolved, add the Kahlúa. Pour into a bowl and leave to cool, stirring now and then to prevent a skin from forming, then chill briefly until just starting to gel. Softly whip the cream with the vanilla and fold it into the mixture. Whisk the egg whites until stiff, gradually add the remaining sugar and whisk to a meringue. Stir a spoonful through the chocolate mixture, then gently fold in the remainder, using a rubber spatula and an up-and-over motion. Pour into six tubby glasses, or eight white wine glasses (leave space if you want to top it with whipped cream), or into 10–12 coffee cups placed on their saucers for serving. Refrigerate until set, decorate and serve. SERVES 6–12.

Almond Meringue Gâteau with Strawberries and Cream

An impressive dessert, always popular and amazingly easy to make.

MERINGUE DISCS
4 extra large egg whites
a good pinch of cream of tartar
250 ml (200 g/7 oz) caster sugar
a few drops of vanilla essence
30 g (1 oz) flaked almonds,
   plus some for topping
cornflour

FILLING
250 g (9 oz) strawberries,
   and a few litchis (optional)
250 ml (9 fl oz) cream
15 ml (1 tbsp) icing sugar
15–30 ml (1–2 tbsp) Amaretto
   liqueur (optional)
a few drops of vanilla essence

Whisk the egg whites to soft-peak stage, add the cream of tartar and whisk until stiff. Gradually whisk in the caster sugar in small, frequent doses, whisking all the time until very stiff. Don't hurry. Fold in the vanilla and almonds. Lightly brush two flat baking trays with oil, line with baking paper, lightly oil the paper, then sprinkle with cornflour, tapping off any excess. Spread a circle of meringue on each tray, making two rounds; they should each be about 20 cm (8 in) in diameter. Sprinkle the extra almond flakes over the top of one round. Bake in the centre of the oven at 120 ˚C (250 ˚F, Gas Mark ½) for 1 hour 15 minutes, then turn off the heat and leave until absolutely cold. Remove the discs from the trays – they should lift off very smoothly, without breaking. If working ahead, store the discs in an airtight container. To make the filling, rinse and hull the strawberries, dry very well and chop. (Litchis – fresh or canned and patted dry – are a lovely addition.) Fold the berries into the cream which has been stiffly whipped with the remaining ingredients. Sandwich the layers, placing the almond-studded disc on the top. Refrigerate for 3–4 hours before serving, to soften it a bit.
SERVES 8.

index

Page numbers for illustrated recipes are in *italic* text.

Glossary of ingredients

Readers in the United Kingdom should convert as follows:
baby marrows = courgettes
brinjals = aubergines, egg plants
cake flour = plain soft flour
cultured sour cream = soured cream
hake = non-oily, delicate and moist, white-fleshed fish

kabeljou and Cape salmon = non-oily, firm and flavoursome white flesh
kingklip = non-oily, white-fleshed fish with large, firm flakes
low-fat smooth cottage cheese = curd cheese
tomato paste = tomato purée or concentrated tomato paste
tomato purée = smooth, thick tomato passata